ABOUT THE AUTHOR

Sharkie Zartman, a former national team member and an all-American from UCLA, is currently a professor at El Camino College in Torrance, California. She coached at the community college level for ten years, winning two state titles, and was inducted into the Beach Volleyball Hall of Fame. Sharkie's husband, Pat, has coached at the club, high school, professional, and international levels and was the USA national volleyball coach in 1974. Their successful Spoilers Volleyball Program won several National Youth titles and produced many collegiate standouts including their daughters, Teri, a UC Irvine setter, and Chrissie, an all-American libero from UCLA.

DEDICATION

To Locke Livernash, my grandfather, who taught me, through example, that there is a lot more to coaching sports than the game. I can still hear his reassuring voice and his laughter and can feel his confidence, empathy, and strength. He is with me always.

ACKNOWLEDGMENTS

There are several people I would like to recognize and thank for their contributions to this book. First and foremost is my husband, Pat, who helped with the technique breakdowns and offered several of the insights and examples in the book. Pat is not only my husband; he is my best friend, confidant, and the best volleyball coach I know. Next are our wonderful daughters, Teri and Chrissie, who have grown up with this sport going on around them and have been great troopers since they were coached by their mom and dad for most of their volleyball careers.

Ken Vick, the director of Velocity Sports Performance, contributed an article entitled "Performance Training: A Professional's Perspective." It is an important article on maximizing athletic potential for coaches, parents, and athletes. Before any athlete, coach, or parent seeks outside training to get an "edge," they must read this article!

Kayo Ryan, one of our "Gold-Star Parents," contributed to the chapter on Coaching and Parents by compiling a piece entitled "From a Parent's Perspective." It is important reading, especially for coaches who at times don't understand where parents are coming from, and for parents to be reminded of what is really important in their child's athletic experience.

Patricia Northington and Kelly Kappen took all the photographs for the book. I am thankful and grateful for their persistence, since some of the pictures we wanted to shoot were difficult to catch on film. I also want to thank Kristen Cooper and Kim Willeman for allowing us to take pictures of their athletes for the book. They and their "models" were most cooperative and fun to work with.

I would like to thank Bernice and Dave Epperson for putting on the Volleyball Festival every year, providing thousands of athletes an opportunity to compete in a prestigious national event that celebrates the athletes and their families. I also want to thank John Kessel from USA Volleyball for his help in reviewing the rules and supplying the demographics.

I want to thank my parents, Mary and Len Boehnert, who allowed me to pursue my passion for sports at a time when most girls were not given any support for wanting to be athletes.

Pat and I are most grateful for all the wonderful kids and families we had an opportunity to coach and work with through the years. Our Spoilers Volleyball family will always be remembered.

I would especially like to thank Holly McPeak for writing the foreword. She is truly an inspiration to everyone who plays this sport.

Last, but not least, I would like to thank my editors, Diana Martin and Michelle Ehrhard, for their insight and direction in development of this book.

TABLE OF CONTENTS

FOREWORD

By Holly McPeak, Three-Time Olympic Volleyball Player
and 2004 Bronze Medalist in Beach Volleyball

I grew up in Manhattan Beach, California, and spent my weekends on the beach with a bunch of different families that would congregate at Seventeenth Street and set up camp. We brought coolers, beach chairs, boogie boards, and volleyballs with us and always had a fun-filled day. My parents would play volleyball and the kids would play games and swim in the ocean, but I started to like to rally the volleyball with anybody who was willing. In just a short time, I was good enough to keep the ball alive and play with some of the adults. I was hooked! My twin brother Gary and my best friend Heather were stuck with me wanting to rally all day long. I could do it hours on end and I was just ten years old! Then I attended my first professional beach volleyball event and it was all over. The athletes were my heroes as I watched them battle it out in the sand all day long. They were super fit, smart athletes, and warriors in my mind. I wanted to be one of them someday.

Growing up in Manhattan Beach, volleyball was *the* sport. I started playing on the middle school team at Center Middle School and I loved it. My first club team was South Bay Volleyball Club, and I learned the basic skills at an early age. Pat Zartman was the head of the club program and taught us good habits from the beginning. I was about five foot six at the time and had really good ball control and basic skills. I thought I would grow some more but at the same time, if I didn't, I wanted to have the type of game that made my teammates better. During the school season, I played on the club and school team, and then beach volleyball all summer. I was constantly challenged by the game and looked forward to every minute I got to play. In high school, I was fortunate enough to play for the powerhouse Mira Costa High School team. I learned discipline, determination, and what it takes to achieve excellence.

The lessons I learned in high school and club have helped me form my work ethic today. I believe in being in the best shape possible and preparing myself for every situation on the court. This type of preparation gives me confidence when I compete and allows me to give it my all when competing. Goals have been an important part of my athletic career and my life. It is important to set goals for yourself in every area of your life and work toward your dreams. Goals are reminders of what we are working for. Dream big, work hard, and go for it!

Youth Volleyball teaches great volleyball drills for every level of player. I still love to do drills that isolate each one of my skills and give me lots of good repetitions so I am confident on the court. Looking back on my career, I realize how important it is to learn how to do things the right way from the beginning. Use this book to help you train the right way and become the best volleyball player or coach you can be.

INTRODUCTION

Volleyball is a great game to play, an exciting game to watch, and a demanding game to coach. Youth volleyball is special due to the exuberance of the kids and parents. It is also special because of the kids' dreams and the vulnerability of their growing psyches. It should be noted, however, that most people are unprepared for the dynamics and demands of coaching youth volleyball and parenting a young volleyball player.

This book was written for the person who wants to be a good coach but has very little experience in working with kids and parents, or who wants to pick up some new ideas and continue to grow as a coach. It is also written for the parent with a child in a volleyball program who wants to better understand the sport, learn how to evaluate the expertise and style of coaches, and help her child enjoy the experience more. This book is also for the athlete who wants to better his game and understand the dynamics going on between parents and coaches.

All young athletes have a basic right to qualified adult leadership. Coaches must take this commitment seriously because of the ultimate impact they may have on each child's future, and parents must be sure to demand coaches who will have a positive impact.

There are no secret formulas that will guarantee success, since all coaches are different and, certainly, all kids are different. There are, however, common guidelines helpful to all youth volleyball coaches, parents, and athletes. This book is meant to be a guide for the conscientious coach and concerned parent who want to have a successful experience and make volleyball a positive experience for the kids. It is my hope that this book will help adults become better coaches and more informed parents and help kids enjoy volleyball to the fullest and learn the lessons it has to offer.

01

THE GAME OF VOLLEYBALL

If William G. Morgan were alive today, he might have trouble recognizing the game he invented more than one hundred years ago. He designed the sport of volleyball for his middle-aged members at the YMCA who needed a less violent and intense game than basketball. The skills in the original game incorporated handball, basketball, and tennis. Since then, volleyball has changed significantly. The game has developed specialized skills different from any other sport, as well as a language of its own. It is a sport that showcases strength, power, agility, speed, and intensity.

Volleyball is the second most popular sport in the world today, surpassed only by soccer. The Federation of International Volleyball (FIVB) acknowledges that there are more than 1.1 billion players worldwide who practice or play the game. According to USA Volleyball (USAV), in the United States there are over 28.7 million participants, with 11.8 million playing indoors, 9.2 million playing on grass, and 7.7 million beach volleyball players. The National Federation of State High School Associations lists girls' volleyball as the third largest girls' team sport behind basketball and track and field. In 2004, over 14,000 schools had girls' teams with almost 400,000 participants. Boys' varsity volleyball is played in 24 states with 1,683 schools fielding teams with over 40,000 athletes. USAV recorded 14,050 girls' club teams and 842 boys' club teams in 2004. The sport continues to grow every year. It's obvious that volleyball is here to stay.

Most of us have played volleyball at school, in the park, or through organized programs and know from firsthand experience what a fun and challenging sport it is. Whether teams consist of two, three, four, or six members, all ages can enjoy the sport from the recreational level up to the most demanding competitive levels. The game has evolved over the years to accommodate various needs and will continue to change in the future.

Basically, the game is played by two teams, separated by a net, who contact a light ball a maximum of three times before it crosses the net to the other team. A match is the best of two out of three games or three out of five games. The rally scoring system is used both indoors and on sand. Although some leagues still play the "old style" of sideout scoring, most are changing to rally scoring because it is faster, easier for the fans to understand and, some believe, more exciting. In rally scoring, a point is awarded to the team that wins the rally. In sideout scoring, only the serving team gets a point for winning the rally. If the receiving team wins the rally it gets a sideout and the next serve.

If the ball hits the floor on the other side of the court within the court boundaries, or the opponents cannot return the ball, the winning team gets a point. It used to be that the serving team received the point, but now the winning team gets a point regardless of who served. The first team to score a designated number of points wins the game or set. The game used to be to 15 points, but with the advent of rally scoring there are many variations. The beach game is played to 21, international and collegiate games are played to 30, club and high school games are played to 25, and a deciding game in a match is played to 15. Confused? You are not alone. The game is in major flux, so continue to go along for the ride and be flexible. We might be playing timed games to 100 next. There are still some leagues that play the game to 15 points with sideout scoring.

The sport can be played almost anywhere: on hardcourts, in sand, on grass, and in water. Wherever a net can be hung and boundaries can be drawn, volleyball can happen. What is especially appealing about this sport is it can be played for a lifetime. USA Volleyball has a senior division at their National Championships for participants over sixty-five years of age. You're never too old, or too young, to enjoy this sport.

THE LANGUAGE OF VOLLEYBALL

In order to teach, coach, or play the game, you must be able to speak and understand the language of volleyball. The following is a list of key terms you should know.

ace: A serve not returned by the opposing team. Some teams celebrate this event by participating in a cheer directed at the opponents that incorporates the clapping of hands and the stamping of feet: "Clap, clap, stamp, stamp, ACE!" or some other variation.

antenna: A thin rod extending above the net at each sideline used to determine the boundary of the net. These are usually not required in recreational settings.

attack: An attempt by the offensive team to end the rally by hitting the ball to the floor of the defensive team.

attacker: A player who spikes or hits the ball over the net.

block: A skill executed above the net by one or more players to prevent a spike from entering their side of the court. It is usually executed with the hands, but the head and face are also legal (but not recommended).

dig: A basic skill used to receive an opponent's attack.

down ball: An attacked ball the blockers judge as not having enough speed or good enough court position to require a block.

foul or fault: Any rule infraction that causes the referee to blow the whistle.

forearm pass: A basic skill where the ball is rebounded off the player's forearms to a desired target.

free ball: A ball returned by the opposing team that cannot be attacked and, instead, is passed over the net.

hit: Another term for an attack or spike.

joust: When the ball comes to rest above the net when two opposing players attempt a block.

kill: An attack not returned by the defense.

libero: A ball-control specialist who wears a different jersey from the other team members. This player may replace any player in the back-row position without counting as a substitution. This player may not attack the ball from above the net or overhand set in front of the ten-foot line.

overhead pass: A basic skill where the ball is contacted above the head with both hands. It can be used on defense, serve receive, and setting.

push pass: An overhead pass where the setting motion is used on service reception or defense. Indoors this technique is allowed on the first contact (serve receive) but is not permitted on the beach.

rally: The time from the start of the serve until the play is ended by a point or a sideout.

rally scoring: A scoring system where a point is scored each time a team wins the rally.

roll: A defensive technique used to contact a low ball out of the body line. The athlete rolls over after the contact to get up quicker.

rotation: When a team earns a sideout, the team moves one position clockwise on the court before the next serve.

serve: A basic volleyball skill used to put the ball into play.

set: An overhead pass directed toward an attacker (hopefully the attacker is on the same team as the setter).

sideout: When the serving team loses the rally and the receiving team gets the ball and the next serve attempt (this is the "old scoring system").

spike: A powerful attack that incorporates jumping and hitting the ball into the opponent's court with one hand.

sprawl: A defensive technique used to retrieve a ball in front of the defender.

tip: An offspeed shot directed by the attacker at holes in the defense (slso called a dink).

THE INDOOR VOLLEYBALL COURT

The volleyball court is nine meters by eighteen meters and divided into two equal playing areas separated by a centerline and a net. The attack line, located three meters from the centerline, prevents the backcourt players from jumping in front of the line to attack the ball or block at the net, since they are not allowed to do so until they are in the front row. Any ball that crosses the net outside the antenna or hits the antenna is considered out of play. (Not all youth programs use antennas because they are not required until the team is playing at the club or high school level.) The net height is seven feet eleven and five-eighths inches for men and seven feet four and one-eighth inches for women. However, the height of the net varies for specific age groups. For junior boys and girls (usually twelve years of age and under), the net may be lowered to seven feet, and for ten years of age and under, the net may be lowered to six feet six inches.

KEY RULES OF THE GAME (INDOORS)

Because the game of volleyball has changed, is changing, and will continue to evolve, keeping up with the rules is challenging. The major governing body for rules is USA Volleyball (USAV), located in Colorado Springs. Every year, a new rule book is issued with the newest changes in the sport, which are incorporated in Junior Olympic Volleyball (club) and Adult Competitions during that year. For a complete book of the rules, go to www.usavolleyball.org.

THE INDOOR VOLLEYBALL COURT

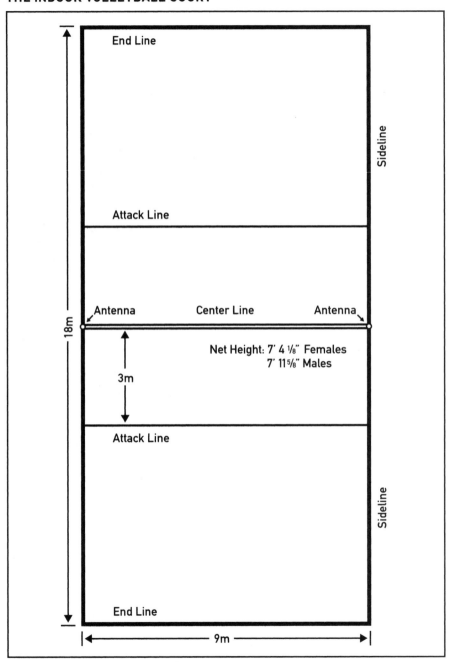

End Line

Sideline

Attack Line

Antenna   Center Line   Antenna

Net Height: 7′ 4 ⅛″ Females
7′ 11⅝″ Males

18m

3m

Attack Line

Sideline

End Line

9m

Most schools and recreational programs eventually catch up, but sometimes there is a time gap where different rules are being played at different levels. The discussion of the rules that follows is a condensed version of the USA Volleyball rules as they apply to Junior Competition. If you are coaching or teaching at a school, you will need to get a copy of the league's rules, since they could be slightly different from the USAV rules. The National Federation of State High School Associations (NFSHSA) and the National Association for Girls and Women in Sports (NAGWS), both listed in the Resources section of this book, are the best sources to get specialized rules for school competitions. The rules for beach volleyball are included in chapter seventeen. As you might imagine, they are much different from the indoor game.

Scoring and Winning

The object of the game is to score 25 points before the other team does. The ball is put into play with the serve, where one team sends the ball over the net to the opposing team. Points are awarded when a team wins a rally by putting the ball down on the opponent's side of the court, or when the other team cannot return the ball. If the serving team wins a rally, it scores a point and continues to serve. If the receiving team wins a rally, it scores a point, rotates, and serves next. A team must win by 2 points, so if the score is 24-24, the winning team must score 2 more points to win.

In a tie-breaking game, which is the third game in a two-out-of-three-game match, or the fifth game in a three-out-of-five-game match, the game is played to 15 points.

In some leagues there is also a point cap so the game can't go on forever, waiting for one team to go up by two. Check your local league's rules to see if there is a cap. If there is no cap, the sky's the limit. Some game scores end up in the 30s. Also, with rally scoring, it is important to note that a team can lose the match on a missed serve. Talk about pressure! Many matches have been lost when a player served the last ball into the net or out-of-bounds.

Team Personnel

A team consists of players, coaches, and, if necessary, trainers and managers who are identified on the team roster. The number of players on a team varies, but most teams consist of between eight and twelve athletes. The maximum is fifteen. Only six can be on the court during the game, and only team members may sit on the bench. There may be overzealous fans who, for some reason, consider themselves a part of the team. Once we saw a team penalized because an athlete's father was sitting on the team bench distracting the players by talking to them and taking pictures. He was a little hard to pick out at first, because he was wearing one of his daughter's spare uniforms.

Each team must submit a roster to the official before the game starts. Only players listed on the roster may play in the match.

The Captain

A team captain must be indicated on the roster. A libero is the only team member who may not be assigned as the floor captain, since he is not on the court all the time. If the captain is not playing, you must designate another player to be the captain. Prior to the match, the captain represents her team in the coin toss and signs the scoresheet. The captain is the only person on the team who may speak to the officials or ask for clarification of a questionable call. This responsibility should be taken into consideration when choosing a captain for the team (no hotheads!).

The Coach

Coaching responsibilities include verifying names and numbers on the rosters, handing in the starting lineup, making substitutions, and calling time-outs. The coach is allowed to give instructions to the players on the court during a match and may stand during a game and move about to speak to the team. Tips for coaching during a match are covered in chapter nine.

The coach is not allowed to use loud or abusive language, make insulting comments to the official or the opposing team, throw objects, display disgust in an overt manner, or interfere with the officiating of the match. For coaches who have trouble in these areas, chapter sixteen offers tips on how to cope with stress, and chapter twelve deals with how to understand and work with officials.

The Players

The athletes must know the rules of the sport and abide by them. They must show sportsmanlike conduct and accept the referee's decisions. The athletes must behave respectfully toward officials, teammates, opponents, and spectators. They usually learn this behavior by watching the coach.

Forbidden Objects

Players may not wear objects that may cause injury or give them an advantager. Athletes may not wear hats or jewelry (such as rings or earrings), and some hair barrettes are not allowed. Players may wear glasses or lenses at their own risk.

Substitutions

Twelve substitutions are allowed in each game (in international volleyball, only six substitutions are allowed). Libero substitutions don't count toward the total. A starting player may enter the game two more times, but only in her previously occupied position. A substitute may enter the game three times in the same position. In other words, if I sub Mary in for Jane, Jane can only go back in Mary's position. More than one substitution is permitted at the same time. You can only make substitutions after a rally is finished.

Libero Substitutions

Each team has the right to designate among the team one libero per game or match. This player only plays in the back row and must wear a different color jersey. The libero is allowed to replace any player in the back row. These replacements are not counted as regular substitutions. They are unlimited, but there must be a rally point scored before the libero returns to the court. The libero can only be replaced by the player he replaced. The coach does not have to call substitution for these replacements.

It is a good idea to keep track of your substitutions so you don't run out or put people in the wrong positions. If you make an improper substitution, you must correct the fault, and the other team gets a point for your error. For these reasons, it is important to keep track of substitutions. The penalties could cost you the match.

Player Positions and Rotations

There are six positions on a volleyball team arranged in order at the time of the service. When the ball is contacted by the server, each team must be completely in the court, except for the server, in two rows of three players. The three players in the front row are considered potential spikers and blockers and are arranged as left front, middle front, and right front. The three players in the back row are arranged as left back, middle back, and right back. The team must be in the correct rotational order before each serve. The illustration on page 10 shows the players in their rotational order. Number one is the right back (the rotational position from which a player serves); number two is the right front; number three is the middle front; number four is the left front; number five is the left back; and number six is the middle back.

After the contact of the serve, the players may move in any direction. At the end of the rally before the next serve, they must return to their original positions if the same server is serving or rotate clockwise if their team's server has changed. With young teams, keeping them in the proper rotational order will be a challenge at first because they sometimes forget where they are supposed to be on the court.

PLAYER POSITIONS

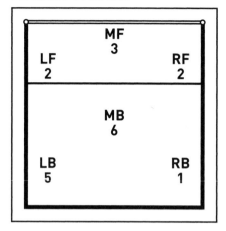

After each side out, the players rotate clock-wise on the court. Each person must be in the correct position until the ball is contacted on the serve.

Rotation Faults

Before the start of each game, the coach has to present the starting lineup of his team on a lineup sheet. The sheet is submitted and signed. Once the lineup has been delivered to the scorer, no changes may be made without a regular substitution. The team's starting lineup indicates the rotational order of the players on the court. This order must be maintained throughout the game.

If the incorrect server serves the ball, the team loses any points scored by the incorrect server, and the other team is rewarded with a point and the next serve.

Overlaps

The position of the players before the service is determined by the position of their feet. Players must be in their correct positions until after contact with the serve, at which time they can move freely to any position on the court. However, the server is exempt and can be anywhere behind the end line. Players must not overlap (extend over) the court area of an adjacent player at the time of service. The overlap rule states that each front-row player must have at least part of a foot closer to the centerline than both feet of the corresponding back-row player (left front vs. left back, middle front vs. middle back, right front vs. right back). Also, each right- or left-side player must have at least part of a foot closer to the right or left sideline than both feet of the middle player in the corresponding row (left front vs. middle front, right front vs. middle front, left back vs. middle back, right back vs. middle back). A violation of the overlap rule results in a point for the other team.

OVERLAP

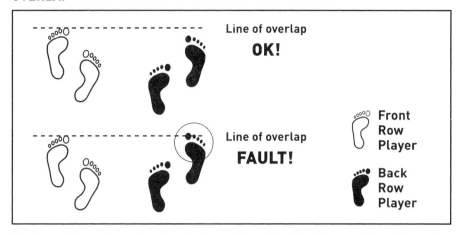

Overlaps on the court are determined by the position of the feet at the same time of the service. This example shows an overlap of a back-row player and a front-row player. Overlaps are illegal because players must be in their correct rotational order before the serve.

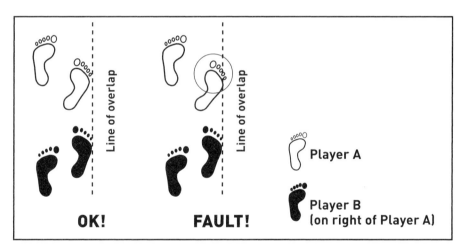

This shows an overlap of players in the same row.

Playing Actions

The rally begins and ends with the referee's whistle. The ball is considered "in" if it touches the floor of the court, including the boundary lines. The ball is "out" when it contacts the floor outside the boundary lines, an object or person out of play (that includes the coach), the antenna, or crosses the net outside the antenna. The ball may be played off the ceiling or other overhead objects above the playing area unless the ball is crossing the net to the opponent's court. A replay is directed if the ball contacts an overhead object less than fifteen feet above the playing area and would have remained playable if the object had not been present (this is the official's decision). A ball is out of play if it contacts the ceiling or overhead objects no matter how high, if over nonplaying areas. However, players should continue playing the ball until they hear a whistle, just in case the official did not see the contact.

Playing the Ball

Each team can contact the ball a maximum of three times in addition to a block. A player may not contact the ball twice in a row, unless the first contact is a block. However, a player may make two contacts in one play, as long as another player touches the ball in between contacts.

If two or three players contact the ball at the same time, it is counted as two or three contacts. If two opponents contact the ball at the same time at the net and the ball stays in play, the team receiving the ball can still have three more contacts. If such a ball goes out, it is the fault of the team on the opposite side on the contact. If a joust occurs above the net with two opposing players causing the ball to come to a rest while blocking above the net, the play continues as if the contacts were instantaneous.

Contacting the Ball

Any part of the body can make contact with the ball, including the feet. It used to be that only above-the-knee contact was allowed. An overhand reception, or "push pass" (receiving the serve or a dig with the hands above the head using the finger pads), is considered legal as long as the ball is not caught or thrown. The forearm pass is still the most popular first contact, but with this recent rule change, we are seeing more overhead receptions. Successive contacts with various parts of the player's body are now permitted in a single action of playing the ball when receiving a serve or a hard-driven ball. This rule has allowed some of the ugliest contacts to be allowed, much to the dismay of fans who do not like this new rule.

Four contacts, a held ball (a catch), double contact (a player contacting the ball twice in succession), and illegal hits (a player contacting the ball in a nonplaying area—another court, benches, or anything marked by the official as such before the match) are considered contact faults. The consequence of a fault is the loss of the rally. If two or more faults are committed successively (one after the other), only the first fault is penalized. If two or more faults are committed by two opponents simultaneously, a double fault is committed and the rally is played over.

Contacting the Net

It is a fault to touch any part of the net or antenna, except for incidental contact by a player's hair or an insignificant contact by a player not involved in the action of playing the ball. This new rule needs to be explained to all sideline, self-appointed referees (usually parents) who happen to have very good eyes when it comes to seeing any infractions by the other team. If the ball is driven into the net, causing the net to touch an opponent, no fault is committed.

Net Play

A ball may touch the net when crossing it, including when the ball is served. A ball driven into the net may be recovered from the net as long as it is one of three contacts allowed. Blockers may contact the ball beyond the plane of the net inside the antennas provided they do not interfere with the opponent's play. Attackers are allowed to follow through beyond the net after the hit provided the ball is contacted within their own playing space or within the plane of the net. Contacts beyond the net are rare occurrences in preteen volleyball because most kids cannot reach over the net until they are older.

A player may reach into or penetrate the opponent's court and space under the net provided it does not interfere with the opponent's play. A player may touch the opponent's court with a foot, feet, or hands provided some part of the hand or foot remains either in contact with or directly above the centerline. If a player's entire foot or hand crosses the centerline during play, it is a fault.

Service Zone

The service zone has been extended to the full width of the back line, meaning the server can serve from wherever she likes along the end line. This can put more pressure on members of the receiving team because they can be attacked from different angles on the serve. This rule also enables the server to get into defensive position quicker.

Service Rules

The serve is the act of putting the ball into play by the right-back-row player. The contact must be with one hand or arm (sorry, no feet). The first team to serve is determined by the official's coin toss before the start of the game. When the serving team wins the rally, the player who served before serves again. When the receiving team wins the rally, players rotate and serve the next ball. The person who moves from the right-front position to the right-back position is the one who will serve the ball.

The server may serve from anywhere across the end line. At the moment of the serve, or takeoff for a jump serve (described in chapter four), the server must be completely in the service zone and not touching the court, including the end line. After the serve, the player may step or land on the line or in the court. The server has only eight seconds after the referee blows the whistle to serve the ball. For USA club rules under age fourteen, if the ball is tossed or released by the server and lands without touching the player, it is considered a service-tossing error. The referee must authorize the service again and the server must execute it within the next five seconds. Only one tossing error is permitted for each service. This is only allowed in the younger competitions and should not be taken advantage of. As the rules change in high school, they will only get one toss. Remind your athletes under fourteen that they only have five seconds to serve after the referee blows the whistle; otherwise, they might take too much time and lose the serve. If the person serves before the whistle is blown, the serve is cancelled and replayed. The ball must be clearly tossed or released. It may not be served out of the hand. The only exception would be in recreational situations where most attempts to serve the ball over the net are accepted.

Serving faults occur if the served ball touches a player of the serving team, fails to go over the net, lands out-of-bounds, or goes over a collective screen (explained below), or when the server foot faults (steps on or over the line when serving). The serve is lost, and the opposing team wins a point and the next serve.

Screening

The serving team may not screen the opponents from seeing the server or the path of the ball. They may not wave their arms, jump, or move sideways when the serve is being executed. They cannot make a collective screen where the server is hidden behind a group of teammates. However, if the players are bunched and they bend over, they are not considered a screen.

Attack Rules

Attack hits are all actions, including a spike, that direct the ball toward the opponent, with the exception of a serve, block, or free ball. An attack hit is completed the moment the ball crosses the vertical line of the net or is touched by a blocker. A back-row player may complete an attack hit at any height from behind the attack line. A libero may not perform an attack hit if, at the moment of the hit, the ball is higher than the top of the net. At the takeoff, the feet of the back-row attacker must neither have touched nor crossed over the attack line (the line located three meters from the net). After the hit, the player may land in front of the attack line. A back-row player may also attack in front of the attack line if, at the moment of contact, any part of the ball is below the top of the net (either the person didn't jump, can't jump, or is very short).

Attack faults occur when a player hits the ball out of bounds, a back-row player attacks from the front zone (as explained above), or a player hits the opponent's serve (you don't see that very often). Also, a player may not complete an attack hit from above the net when the ball is overhand set by a libero in front of the three-meter attack zone.

Blocking Rules

Blocking is a deflection of the ball from the opponent by a player or players close to the net reaching higher than the net. Remember, a block does not count as one of the three hits allowed. Consecutive contacts may occur by one or more blockers provided the contacts are made during one action.

Blocking faults occur when the blocker touches the net or touches the ball in the opponent's space before or simultaneous with the opponent's attack hit. Back-row players are not allowed to participate in a block. Also, a blocker may not block the opposing team's serve. This would allow a "vertically enhanced" team to have one more advantage than it already has (some school programs still allow this, however).

Time-outs

Each team is allowed two thirty-second time-outs per game. During this time, the team players must leave the playing court and go to the free area near the bench. Use your time-outs wisely, since they are short and infrequent.

Changing Sides

After each game, the teams change sides. In the deciding game when a team reaches 8 points, the teams change sides remaining in the same rotational positions. Basically, at the conclusion of a game, or at 8 points in the deciding game, all players on the court must go to the end line (indicated by the referee's motion). Then, when the referee indicates (by crossing one arm in front of her body and one behind), teams move counterclockwise to the other side of the court. Any players or coaches on the bench follow behind the team.

Injuries

If an injury should occur, the referee will stop the game and the rally will be replayed. Thirty seconds is allowed for the player to return to the game, a time-out to be called, or a substitution to be made. An injured player who cannot continue playing should be substituted legally. If this is not possible, the team is entitled to make an "exceptional" substitution. This means that any player who is not on the court at the time of the injury, except the libero or his replacement player, may substitute into the game for the injured player. If this type of substitution is made, the injured player is *not* allowed to re-enter the match.

Dealing With Infectious Disease

With the concern of infectious diseases being spread through contact with blood, some important guidelines must be followed by all teams when dealing with a bleeding player.

If an official notices a player is bleeding, she will stop the game, and the player must leave the game for evaluation or treatment. If the player cannot return, a substitution must be made. If the player returns, the injury must be covered. If the uniform has blood on it, it must be changed. Players can have numbers other than their original ones, as long as the numbers are not the same as the other players on the team. As a coach, it would be a good idea to carry an extra uniform with you so you do not have to bench a player because of blood on a uniform. If there is blood on the playing surface or equipment (especially the ball), the game will be stopped and the area will be cleaned. These measures are meant to protect everyone from the slight possibility of contracting an infectious disease from coming into direct contact with blood.

Misconduct

Have you ever seen an official flash a yellow card, red card, or both? These cards are significant because they represent penalties for misconduct on the part of the athletes, spectators, or coaches. Most of the time, they are directed at the coach. Three categories of individual behavior are classified as misconduct and may be sanctioned by the official. They are indicated by flashing a yellow or red card, or a combination of the two. Each card indicates a different infraction, detailed below.

YELLOW CARD
Unsportsmanlike Conduct: Arguing, intimidating behavior, threats.
Sanction: Misconduct warning. Penalty.

RED CARD
Rude Conduct: Expressing contempt.
Sanction: Expulsion from the game.

Offensive Conduct: Foul language or gestures, extremely offensive or repeated rude conduct.

Sanction: Disqualification from the match.

Although only team members may be sanctioned by the referee, spectators, including parents who misbehave, may be asked to leave the site by the tournament personnel. You might want to explain what these cards mean and the sanctions they indicate. Officials don't leave home without these cards.

Assigning Line Judges and Umpires

As a coach, you will most likely have to assign athletes from your team to help with the officiating. You will need to supply two linesmen and perhaps one umpire for the matches you have been assigned to officiate. Make sure they know their responsibilities.

The linesmen must call the ball in or out, and any touches they see before the ball went out of bounds. They must stay alert during the games and not talk to their friends. Also, they must hold their ground when people in the crowd start to question their calls. If needed, the umpire allows substitutions to take place and watches for net violations, touches on the block, and foot faults. Most of the time, the head official is supplied by the tournament, but in the event this is not the case, you, as coach, might be asked to be the head referee. Make sure you know the rules and the referee signals. You can find them in chapter twelve.

Official Score

You will have to assign one or two people to help keep score. Sometimes, keeping score is just keeping track of points with a flip chart or scoreboard. You may also have to teach your athletes how to record the game on the official scoresheet. Make sure you and your athletes know how to use whatever scoresheet is required. Most leagues will not allow teams to play unless they have at least one person who knows how to do the "official score."

Summary

As far as the rules are concerned, my best advice is to stay open and don't get too comfortable with any rule change or scoring system. Whether it's going to quarters, playing to 130 points, freezing scores, raising or lowering the net, shortening or lengthening the court, or changing the size and color of the ball, remember that volleyball is a great game that can be played for a lifetime.

02 VOLLEYBALL PROGRAMS

There are many programs available for kids to learn and play volleyball. To understand the purpose of each program, they must be clearly defined. To assume all programs are alike is only asking for trouble. Parents need to know which program will best suit their children.

There are five programs for children to participate in: recreational, instructional, competitive, and two combination programs, instructional–recreational and instructional–competitive. There is no such thing as a recreational–competitive program for kids. I'll explain why at the end of this chapter.

RECREATIONAL PROGRAMS

The meaning of the word *recreate* means "to give new life to." For a child, this means to play. Long before adult-organized recreation programs, kids were recreating on their own. They made up games with their own rules and played for hours on end. When it comes to volleyball, all kids need is a net and a ball. They can improvise the rest.

In adult-organized recreation programs, the emphasis should be on participation and fun. "Everyone plays" is always a good clue that the program will be recreational. When it comes to children's recreational programs, it is a good idea to use a light ball and make the court smaller. In mini-volleyball, you can put two youth courts on a regular-sized volleyball court. The net is also lower depending on the size and age of the children. Teams can be made up of two, three, or four people. Emphasis is on movement and participation. The skills of the game are shown, but teaching is not the primary concern of a purely recreational program. The participants learn by doing and enjoy the sport in its most primitive form.

If you want to get involved in a recreational program, set up a court in your yard, at a park, or at the beach and invite kids to come down and play volleyball. If the experience is fun, some kids will be motivated to move to the next level.

MINI-VOLLEYBALL COURT

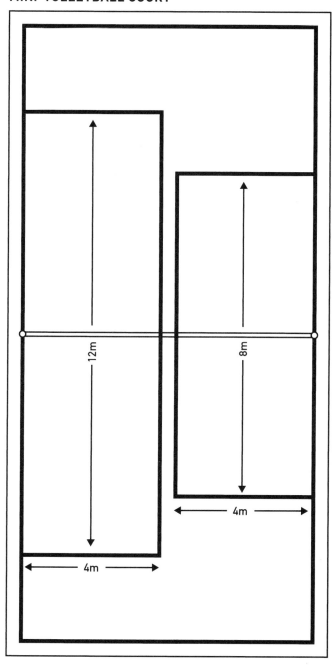

A regular volleyball court can be turned into two narrow courts for youth volleyball. They can both be the same size, or one can be shorter for the youngest players. Teams can consist of two, three, or four players.

02

INSTRUCTIONAL PROGRAMS

An instructional program is where skill progression is taught and the participants learn the rules and strategy of the game. Some kids do not want to be in an instructional program—they just want to play. They should stay in a recreational program until they are ready and want to learn the game correctly.

Teaching volleyball skills is very demanding. In order for you to be effective, you must know how to break the skills down to a level that kids can easily understand and master, and you must have a great deal of patience. You must also be a motivator, since learning volleyball can be very frustrating; kids usually experience a lot of failure before they succeed.

If you want to teach volleyball, you can offer classes or clinics either privately or through schools or recreational programs.

COMPETITIVE PROGRAMS

Any program that has tryouts and makes cuts is a competitive program. To compete, athletes must earn playing time. We suggest that kids do not enter a competitive program until they have strong self-esteem and their parents are aware of the nature of competitive sports. Playing time is determined by the coach, and all coaches have different criteria for how much time an athlete is on the court during the game and in what role. If you are ready to coach in a competitive program, you must be clear what your philosophy is (see chapter ten) and have solid criteria for player selections and playing time allotments. In a competitive program, the coach tries to make the team successful. The effort to win is emphasized, but the eventual outcome is not. Winning and losing is not what competing is all about. It is about getting the best out of the players and the team. It's about striving to reach one's potential. It's about training hard to be your best. Coaches at this level need to know how to utilize their athletes so they can be successful and help the team.

A purely competitive program usually does not involve a lot of instruction. It is assumed the players already have the skills and are ready to help a team be successful. Most of the work done by the coach is in the areas of team strategy and motivation. Most kids are not ready for a purely competitive situation because they still need a lot of work on the basics, and some kids are not ready to earn a position.

COMBINATION PROGRAMS

As you can see from these program definitions, there needs to be some overlap in order to have programs for all concerned. Most youth programs are combination programs that are either instructional–recreational or instructional–competitive. These two pro-grams add the instructional component, while allowing the children to also play the game or compete.

INSTRUCTIONAL–RECREATIONAL

This type of program combines learning and playing together. The amount of time spent doing each depends on the age and maturity level of the kids. When kids are very young, a greater amount of time would be spent on play, with less time spent on learning. This type of program is fun to be involved in because you can see the kids enjoy the game more as they become proficient at the skills. There is also a lot of room for creativity. The keys to this type of program are to teach the skills correctly and maximize participation. The outcomes of the games in terms of winning or losing are minimized.

Here are some tips on how to coach an instructional–recreational program:

1. For young kids, get as many balls as you can, and be sure they are soft. Kids won't want to contact the ball if it hurts their arms.

2. Turn skills into games instead of drills. For example, when teaching serving, have one side serve and the other side be targets. The targets can be anywhere they want on the court, but they must not move. When a server hits a target, they change places. Kids will laugh and scream and have a great time, and will probably make a lot more serves than if you just had them serve it over the net in a boring drill.

3. Teach hitting first. This will hook them into learning the other skills once they realize they can't hit until they can serve, pass, and set. Spiking is the skill everyone enjoys the most, so why not start off with that?

4. Experiment with mini-volleyball. One of the problems with learning volleyball is that there are six people on both sides of the court and only one ball being played. This means some kids might not get to contact the ball very often, if at all, and will end up getting frustrated and bored. So why not cut the teams and the court in half? This can be easily done with a piece of chalk.

Put four kids on each court and let them play all four positions. The person who is middle front will be the setter, the other three will pass and hit, and they will rotate clockwise as they normally would. Not only does this allow more contacts for the kids, it allows more kids on one court (sixteen instead of twelve). The teams can play the team directly across from them, or for an even bigger challenge, the one diagonal from them (a crosscourt game). As the teams get stronger, the number can be cut to three, then two.

5. You choose the teams and make them different each time. Do not allow kids to choose their own teams. Psychology books are full of stories of kids being chosen last for teams in their physical education classes and the resulting damage to their self-esteem. Believe it or not, it can leave a permanent impression. Were you ever the last one chosen? (I still haven't recovered.)

You can organize the teams any way you wish, just as long as you mix it up often. Most coaches have stronger players on one court and weaker players on another, but you will find out a lot about your kids if you mix levels periodically. Have the weaker players play with the stronger ones. Usually, the weaker players will try harder and be more motivated, and the stronger players will learn how to help others and be good role models. Remember, part of what kids need to learn about sports is how to work with everyone, not just their friends or the best athletes.

6. Have them practice skills sometimes without a ball. Turn footwork and skills into a choreographed routine. This will help get it into their muscle memory, which will make it more of a reaction.

7. Be enthusiastic! Kids can sense whether or not you enjoy what you are doing. If you love volleyball (and you must to put yourself in this situation), share it with the kids. Get out there at times and be a part of the workout. Be an example. You don't need to show off, but it helps if you can participate enough to let them see your enthusiasm and enjoyment for the game.

8. Ignore mistakes. Reward effort. No matter what level you teach or coach, this will keep you from turning into a nag. Kids will try a lot harder if they know they will be rewarded for doing something correctly vs. getting yelled at for doing something wrong.

If you want to get involved in an instructional–recreational program, you can contact your city's parks and recreation department, the closest YMCA or YWCA, or start a private program wherever you can get a facility and a permit. Also, physical education classes at schools are a challenging variation of an instructional–recreational program because the kids "have to be there." A physical education teacher must have good discipline and be a motivator in addition to being a good teacher.

INSTRUCTIONAL-COMPETITIVE

A combination program of instruction and competition is the most challenging program to be involved in. You must be an exceptional teacher when it comes to teaching techniques, because most games are won and lost at the fundamental level. The team that makes the most mistakes loses. As coach, you must also deal with the competitive element, which incorporates making some hard decisions about team personnel, positions, playing time, etc. You must also be able to communicate with parents, which can be difficult at times, because they have a totally different perception from the coach (see chapter thirteen).

02

If you want to work at this level, club or school competition are the two programs that can be either competitive or instructional-competitive. With younger teams, you need a solid instructional element. We have seen teams both at the club and school level that were thrown into competition without first learning the skills. Obviously, it was very frustrating to watch. How can a coach expect a team to win if they don't have skills? For this reason, the best coaches should be at the lower levels. To start a club program, contact the nearest USA Junior Olympic Volleyball regional office in your area. In order to coach in a high school program, you should have experience in teaching or coaching and ideally have a degree in education or physical education. At the junior high or elementary level, even though you don't necessarily need a degree, you must be able to teach the game properly.

Even though this level is the most challenging, it can also be the most rewarding if done properly. Kids can learn a lot of important lessons at the competitive level that they can take with them long after they are done with volleyball. However, it is also at this level that a lot of damage can be done. Part of it stems from the kids being in the program at the wrong time.

RECREATIONAL VS. COMPETITIVE

Recreational and competitive programs are in direct opposition to one another. You *cannot* run both at the same time. Before you get into a program, you must decide what is best for you and make sure the kids and parents understand what the program is all about. In recreation programs, everyone plays, and the emphasis is on participation and fun. In competitive programs, the players earn a spot and try to make the team successful. There is no common ground. Coaches get into trouble when they don't define their program, don't communicate what their program is about, or change their program as they go along. I know of one coach who told the players and parents that the kids were all going to play and have fun, so it was assumed this was going to be an instructional-recreational program. After collecting five hundred dollars for each child, he changed his mind and turned it into a competitive program when he decided his team might have a shot at winning a title. He no longer played everyone and started pressuring his team to win. Obviously, some of the parents were very upset.

Problems will always arise if you are coaching a recreational team and turn it into a competitive situation, or if you are coaching a competitive team with some kids and parents who have a recreational mindset. At the onset, you must communicate with the athletes and parents which type of program you are running and stick to it. If it does not suit their needs, they should be allowed to find a program that does. Unfortunately, a lot of kids get into a competitive program by mistake. Usually, these kids and their parents become unhappy because the kids don't get to play enough and end up discouraged.

Programs for the youngest kids should be recreational and instructional. The transition to a competitive situation should be the athlete's choice, not the parents' or the coach's. There are some kids who will never want to be in competitive sports, but they should still have the opportunity to play. We need both recreational and competitive programs for kids, but they should be separate and distinct from each other. Otherwise, there will always be kids who are left out and unhappy, and coaches and parents who will be in conflict.

KIDS, AGE, ABILITY, AND OTHER DIFFERENCES 03

There are major problems in store for the youth volleyball coach who assumes all kids are alike. Your task is to be able to deal with every type of child and treat them fairly. This presents some incredible challenges since volleyball is a team sport and you must get different kinds of kids to work together toward common goals. We can't even get adults to do this unless we pay them, and most of the time, that doesn't work.

WHAT ARE THE SIMILARITIES IN KIDS?

When it comes to playing volleyball or any other sport, the only two things kids really have in common are that they want to play and they want to have fun. There are no other universal common characteristics. It is up to you to find out how each of your athletes are different, respect them for who they are, and find some way to make the volleyball experience enriching for each child. Coaches who treat kids like miniature adults or try to turn every child into a superstar are not doing their jobs.

WHAT ARE THE DIFFERENCES IN KIDS?

From our coaching experience, we've noted some major forces that are responsible for most of the differences we see in kids. They are physical, personality, and intellectual differences, family influences, and maturity.

PHYSICAL DIFFERENCES

Physical differences important to a youth volleyball coach are body type, quickness, power, and height.

Body Type

Body type normally refers to the ratio of lean body mass to fat. Lean body mass is muscle and bone. Four body types are usually identified. One is the thin child who has a slight amount of lean body mass and fat. Usually this child appears weak and fragile. Another type is a child with a higher ratio of fat to lean body mass. This child is carrying extra baby fat that could make any sport more challenging. The third body type is the child with a higher ratio of lean body mass to fat. These children appear very muscular. The fourth and most common body type is an even amount of lean body mass to fat. These are your physically normal kids. When coaches first evaluate kids on body types, the ones they normally gravitate toward are those with the extra muscle mass. They assume (sometimes incorrectly) that these athletes will be the most successful and help the team the most. But the emotional and intellectual makeup of a child will sometimes cancel out body type. Also keep in mind that body types usually change with maturation. We have seen very thin, fragile kids fill out and grow muscular, overweight children lose their excess body fat and become commanding athletes, and muscular children who appeared to have every advantage in the world not use their advantages. So when it comes to body types, take it with a grain of salt. There are other characteristics that are far more important.

Quickness

Quickness is another physical characteristic important in volleyball. How quick a person is depends on two things: reaction time and movement speed. *Reaction time* is defined as the amount of time it takes from when a person senses something to when he starts to react to it. If you were driving a car, it would be the amount of time it would take from when you saw a red light to when you actually put your foot on the brake. *Movement speed* is how fast the actual move was. For example, once you started to brake, how long it would take to stop the car. So when you start to look at quickness, you need to know there are actually two parts to it. Volleyball requires a person to react and move quickly. When working with kids, it takes a while for them to develop these reactions. They might see a ball coming to them, but the reaction is delayed because their quickness is too slow at first. I remember working with my team when they were seven, and the ball would come toward them and they wouldn't move at all, or maybe they would move, but only at the neck. Quickness takes time when a person has to coordinate it with a ball. When working with kids, be patient. Soon it will become a reaction.

Power

Power is defined as strength and speed combined. Some kids have a lot of power, even though they don't appear to be strong. We had one girl on our team with the skinniest arms you've ever seen. Surprisingly, she was one of our most effective spikers and had a killer jump serve. Don't assume kids don't have power if they don't have a lot of muscle mass. There's a lot more to power than muscle size.

Height

Height is genetically determined. Unlike other physical characteristics, it cannot be trained. Being tall does have its advantages, but it is only one characteristic of a volleyball player. If the person has height, but no heart, mind, quickness, or power and very little skill proficiency, she will be of little use to you and the team. Work on developing the other trainable characteristics. Don't make the mistake of choosing only tall kids for your team.

PERSONALITY DIFFERENCES

A child's personality and how you interact with him can make a huge difference in how successful the child is and whether you have a positive coaching/teaching experience. Personality, in a nutshell, is how a child consistently behaves. There are some areas that, as a coach, you can change, and others you can merely react to.

As researchers are learning more about personality, they are discovering that certain personality traits are genetically set. Traits like emotional expressiveness and motivational drive cannot be changed and therefore must instead be acted on. The personality differences may become apparent when your kids start to compete. Certain kids seem like born competitors and others seem more passive. All children want to succeed, but they will sometimes show it in different ways. I remember one athlete on my college team who was a good athlete, always did her job, but she never looked like she was trying. This was upsetting to me because I was exactly the opposite as an athlete. It wasn't until my husband reminded me of these set personality differences (he is a psychology teacher) that I understood she was just being herself. To ask her to change her personality because I was different would be totally unfair and probably would make her a lesser player. The bottom line is you can't turn a passive athlete into a born competitor.

You need all personality types to make your team balanced. Appreciate the kids you have and work at developing them into the best team and individuals they can be.

Sometimes, the best competitors happen to be the quietest kids. They have the "coolest heads" and will keep some of the other players from getting out of control.

In terms of personality traits that can be changed, this requires discipline. Chapter eleven deals with discipline and is required reading for every coach.

INTELLECTUAL DIFFERENCES

How kids process information is obviously an important consideration for a coach. There is a lot to learn when a child starts to play volleyball, and whether they can understand what you say, and retain it, is an important consideration. Most kids are visual learners. They learn more by seeing than hearing. Keep this in mind when you want them to remember something. Give them a visual image. Demonstrate the technique by using either yourself or one of the athletes. You can also show them a picture, drawing, or videotape of a person doing the skill correctly and videotape your athletes.

Interest level is another factor when you consider intellectual differences. If they don't want to learn anything, they won't. Kids who are forced into volleyball by their parents will be a challenge because their hearts won't be in it. They would much rather be doing something else.

FAMILY INFLUENCES

Besides all the varied genetic differences, there are also several different environmental influences that affect children, starting with their families. Some of your athletes will come from a home with two parents and at least one brother or sister. Others will come from single-parent families, have a stepfamily, be raised by a relative, have no siblings, or have too many to keep track of. The possibilities of these varied families and how they affect a child are endless. The only thing you can do is realize most children are coming from different family environments, and they all have a different perspective based on what they have learned at home. You must keep this in mind when making generalizations about how things are. This could be very different from what they have learned and believe. Be very specific when you make rules based on values. Let them know these are the "team's rules." A simple rule might be, "This team will not allow any offensive language." A child will accept and comply, even if everyone in his family cusses at will.

Children also learn from their families about responsibility, taking criticism, how to work together, and how to share. If they are not learning these lessons from their families, you have an opportunity to teach them.

MATURITY

Another important consideration in dealing with kids and differences is maturity. Kids mature at different times and at different rates. Coaches who work with very young children will sometimes get discouraged because they have unsuccessfully tried everything to get a child to learn a certain skill. In most cases, it's not that the coach isn't teaching the skill properly. It's just that the child is not ready to learn it yet. There are several neural pathways in the brain that have to be trained and conditioned before a movement pattern can be performed successfully. Consider how difficult it is for a baby to learn how to walk. Some parents labor over teaching their child to walk before he is ready. Then one day, for no particular reason, the kid just does it. Remember this when you have a young athlete who is having trouble mastering a skill. Be patient and reward effort. Her time will come.

Maturation also presents its problems with physical development. As children get closer to puberty, their bodies will start to change at varying rates. You could have a team of twelve-year-olds whose height could vary as much as a foot. The kids whose bodies are growing at a very fast rate will sometimes have trouble adapting to the new changes in their bodies and may appear very awkward. Also, during puberty, physical changes start to become apparent between boys and girls. Up until puberty, the physical differences between boys and girls are minimal. Now, these differences can present all sorts of challenges, especially if you coach or teach a mixed group of girls and boys. Girls usually mature first and will be taller and stronger than most boys at the same age. When boys catch up, they will pass girls in the area of strength because they have more muscle, which will start to develop when the boys start to secrete testosterone. When girls start to secrete estrogen and progesterone, which they need for the menstrual cycle, you never know what will happen. This can affect their personality because of unpredictable mood swings. Coaching kids at this stage is very challenging because of the different changes puberty causes in youngsters at different times. A knowledgeable coach is aware of this area of maturation and puberty and is empathetic and ready to deal with this challenge. Remember that you, too, went through puberty once.

Besides genetics, family, and maturation, you also have media influences, school, friends, relatives, religion, culture, other sports and coaches, social status, and so on. All of these influences affect children in different ways. If, after reading about these differences, you still think all kids are alike and you are going to treat them all the same, do yourself and everyone else a favor and don't coach.

WHEN IS THE RIGHT AGE TO START VOLLEYBALL?

A common question that comes up when discussing youth volleyball is, "At what age are the kids ready to start playing volleyball?" That is really up to the child. When they start mimicking the game is when they will start to play it. Years ago, my husband, Pat, and I were at a volleyball tournament with our daughter, Teri, when she was two years old, and a concerned father came over to us and said there was something wrong with our daughter. We looked down and she had her foot over her head and it appeared to be stuck. Pat dislodged her foot, and just after he had done this she pulled her foot back over her head. We looked around the gym, and there was a team practicing the shoulder roll, a defensive technique where players roll on the floor and pull their legs over their shoulders. Teri was trying it on her own, and even though she was getting stuck, she was having a great time. A lot of kids actually start playing volleyball before adults and coaches are even aware of it. They find a ball or a balloon and rebound it against a wall, or find a partner and play a game over a couch or a chair. Our kids started with a balloon ball and would play all the time around the house. I can't tell you how many times we got hit in the head with a ball. Young kids will mimic what they like; they have active imaginations and will find a way to play whatever game they want. If you have a child who is around the game and is expressing an interest, get a balloon and play one-on-one. Make it fun.

When a child is ready to learn the game is another matter. As mentioned earlier, the skills in volleyball are difficult to learn because it is a rebound sport requiring coordination, timing, and skill. A child will usually be able to perform a variety of motor skills by the age of five or six, but the combination of tracking a ball and rebounding it with a body part is very challenging. When you combine this with a relatively short attention span, you can see why teaching kids at this young age is difficult. A good rule of thumb is to introduce skills to kids when they want to learn them with the understanding that the emphasis should be on fun and trying to do the basic skills correctly. By age eight, most children can start to learn the skills of the game. They are physically ready and have enough of an attention span to learn something new.

There are three stages, corresponding with approximate ages, most children go through when you consider interest and motivation for participating in a sport.

STAGE ONE: AGES FOUR THROUGH EIGHT

In this beginning stage, the child is most interested in having fun. That is why she is playing in the first place. She is not participating to win; she just wants to play. If you are working with kids this young, it's your job to keep it fun. I remember when I took my kids to their first tournament when they were seven years old; when they won their first game, they were upset because they had to stop playing the game.

STAGE TWO: AGES NINE THROUGH THIRTEEN

As children get older, some of them get more competitive. They want to get a shiny trophy or a sparkling medal. The first time a child receives one of these trinkets is very special, and he usually will be motivated to get more. Sports must be fun for kids, and they are usually willing to pay more of a price to win. They will be more open to learning how to do the skills correctly if it will help them to be more successful. We know of one mother who was thrilled because her daughter's coach said their only goal for the year was to have fun. She was pleased to hear this because she thought her daughter would be happy in this situation and not experience any stress. The coach was true to his word and played everyone equally and just emphasized fun (a recreational program). They lost most of their games. To the mother's astonishment, her daughter was devastated. I told the mother that perhaps her child was turning into a competitor and was willing to give up a little bit of fun in order to be more successful. As children cross this line, they begin to realize life's rewards do not come easily. That is what competition is all about. Some kids cross this line early, others later, and some never. Remember, not all kids need to be competitors in sports, and they should never be forced across this line by a coach or a parent. Unfortunately, this happens way too often. Children who don't cross into competition should still be able to enjoy sports at the recreational level. They can still benefit from the sport's physical demands and stay in shape in the same way. We hear stories all the time about kids who were forced into competition before they were ready and now hate sports and won't do anything active because they had such a bad experience when they were young. YMCAs and recreational departments have great programs for kids who want to play volleyball and have fun.

STAGE THREE: AGES FOURTEEN THROUGH EIGHTEEN

In the final years of childhood, we see many athletes who are not as concerned with winning as they are with achieving their personal best. The trophies and medals start to take on less meaning. What they are really after is just how good they can be. As a coach, working with kids at this stage can be very rewarding. However, it takes a lot of discipline, work, and understanding to get athletes close to achieving their potential. Even at this stage, fun and reward are there, but they are not the driving force. At this level, athletes will tell you the reason they compete is because they love it.

PLAYING OPPORTUNITIES FOR DIFFERENT AGES

At the earliest stage, there are several opportunities for children to play volleyball. Get a light ball, set up a boundary line, a rope for a net, and play. The smaller the child, the smaller the boundaries and the lower the rope. Play one-on-one and emphasize movement to the ball. Don't worry about emphasizing skills, just play. Mini-volleyball (see chapter two) is a good way to introduce the structure of the game with rules and more than one kid on each side.

In the middle stage, kids are ready to learn the skills. There are several recreational and YMCA programs for young children to learn the game. Some physical education classes will start to teach the fundamentals as part of a structured program. There are also competitive programs in clubs and schools for kids who are ready to start competing against other children their age. Mini-volleyball is another opportunity for kids in the middle stage.

At age thirteen and up, most schools offer interscholastic competitions and kids can try out and play for their school teams. Many schools also have teams for younger athletes—sometimes as young as third graders. Most of the time, these programs tend to be competitive, with each school trying to win its respective league. There are also many Junior Olympic Clubs that have tryouts for different level teams starting at this age and sometimes younger. Keep in mind that there are several recreational programs available for kids who are not ready for the rigorousness of competition. All kids who want to play should be able to do so in an environment where they feel comfortable.

TRAINING ATHLETES AT DIFFERENT AGES

Here are seven areas in which the individual differences of kids in different stages of development must be addressed in regard to volleyball training:

TRAINING KIDS AGES FOUR THROUGH EIGHT

Athletic Abilities: They have basic motor skills but have trouble tracking objects, especially one traveling fast (like a volleyball). Concentrate on movement to the ball. Start with smaller, slower movements and, once the kids are successful, work up to faster, longer movements.

Attention Span: The range is very short, and it comes and goes. When working with this age group, make sure they are looking at you when you are talking or demonstrating a skill.

Interest Level: Remember, this age group is most interested in having fun. So make volleyball fun!

Emotional Maturity: This area is highly variable. A lot depends on home environment and genetic predispositions. Some kids will still be very attached to their parents. Be sensitive, but try to concentrate on volleyball, not behavior.

Comprehension and Retention: Kids this age are visually oriented. Showing is more important than telling. Show skills and techniques by doing them yourself, using a kid to demonstrate, or using a picture or a video.

Best Playing Opportunities: Play should take place with parents and friends on makeshift courts. Recreational programs are available for kids this age at parks and local YMCAs. More mini-volleyball opportunities need to be available for this age group.

Skills Needed: Movement to the ball is the major area that must be emphasized. Basic skills can be introduced but not overly emphasized.

TRAINING KIDS AGES NINE THROUGH THIRTEEN

Athletic Abilities: Kids are stronger and quicker than before, enabling them to hit the ball with more force for serving and spiking. Tracking objects becomes easier, and they can move to the ball more quickly. Some girls will be going through puberty, affecting their agility as they adapt to their changing bodies.

Attention Span: This should be longer than the previous stage but still variable depending on circumstances. You must work at getting and keeping their attention by enhancing communication skills (see chapter eleven).

03

Interest Level: Volleyball still has to be fun, but some kids will start to exhibit a competitive attitude. If this is a recreational program, the competitive kids must understand what recreation is all about. If it is a competitive program, the recreational-mindset kids need to be reminded what competition is all about. Remember, there is no such thing as a recreational–competitive program (check back to chapter two).

Emotional Maturity: By this age, kids usually have outgrown their attachment to their parents. Now, you need to worry about their friends (peer pressure) because they may have more influence than the parents and the coach combined.

Comprehension and Retention: Kids are still visually oriented at this stage but will listen more. They are becoming masters of voice inflection. Watch how you say things.

Best Playing Opportunities: Play should take place through recreational programs that also provide instruction. Some kids will be ready for competitive programs.

Skills Needed: The basic skills of forearm pass, set and spike, and the sidearm serve are the skills most needed at this level.

TRAINING KIDS AGES FOURTEEN THROUGH EIGHTEEN

Athletic Abilities: Girls are reaching their prime in terms of maturation. They are usually very strong and have hit their peak height at about sixteen years of age. Boys at this stage are usually starting puberty and may go through an awkward stage. Boys usually peak in their maturation at age eighteen or nineteen.

Attention Span: Usually this is pretty long, unless a member of the opposite sex comes into view.

Interest Level: Volleyball should still be fun, but more effort is put into winning, and some are interested in achieving their personal best in the sport.

Emotional Maturity: This is still variable, especially in girls. Be prepared for anything.

Comprehension and Retention: This is usually very strong; they know and understand what you want them to do. Getting them to do it is something else.

Best Playing Opportunities: This depends on their interest. Recreational programs are still available and more competitive opportunities open up. School and clubs are good avenues for competition.

Skills Needed: All the previous skills are needed, plus the overhand serve, the jump serve, blocking, digging, sprawling and rolling, and the strategies of team play.

03

04

BASIC SKILLS

Correct movement patterns and the mastery of fundamental skill techniques are the foundations, cornerstones, and keys to ball control and success in the game of volleyball. The skills of serving, passing, setting, digging, spiking, and blocking are unlike any other sports skills, so there is usually no carryover from other sports. In fact, other sports skills may actually limit a child's ability to learn a volleyball skill because of preconditioned motor responses. Quickness, power, and agility will facilitate learning these skills, but a coach must start from scratch when working with children. This takes time, knowledge, and patience.

To control the ball, it is essential for players to operate from a balanced position. Learning correct movement patterns makes this possible. From the proper position, skills that are executed correctly give players control of the ball and the best chance for success. However, skills don't just happen. They must be learned through repetition and feedback.

Since movement patterns and basic techniques are so important, they must be taught to and later reinforced with players of all ages and abilities. The only difference in instruction is the speed and precision demanded and the pace of the ball.

BASIC MOVEMENT AND FOOTWORK

All volleyball players must be able to go to the ball with efficient footwork. The basic movement patterns must become second nature. Some coaches teach skills before they teach movement and become frustrated when kids don't move to the ball. Remember, volleyball players are not magnets. The ball does not automatically come to them. They must move to the ball.

FOOTWORK PATTERNS

Since all volleyball players must be able to go to the ball with efficient footwork, this simple warm-up routine is an excellent way to make the basic movement patterns second nature to the athletes. Besides teaching athletes to move in all directions to the ball, it is also an excellent warm-up for the legs.

PART ONE: HOP STEP

1. Take a step forward with the right foot; in rapid succession, leap/hop forward to a balanced position landing in a left-foot-right-foot succession.
2. Take a step backward with the right foot; rapidly leap/hop backward to a balanced position landing in a left-foot-right-foot succession.
3. Take a step forward with the left foot; rapidly leap/hop forward to a balanced position landing in a right-foot-left-foot succession.
4. Take a step backward with the left foot; rapidly leap/hop backward to a balanced position landing in a right-foot-left-foot succession.

PART TWO: SLIDE STEP

5. Step laterally with the right foot; step with the left foot and close to the right foot; step with the right foot to a balanced position with both feet under the corresponding shoulders.
6. Step laterally with the left foot; step with the right foot and close to the left foot; step with the left foot to a balanced position with both feet under the corresponding shoulders.

PART THREE: OPEN HOP STEP

7. Repeat step one.
8. Turn to the right and step 180 degrees with the right foot; in rapid succession leap/hop to a balanced position landing in a left-foot-right-foot succession.
9. Turn to the left and step 180 degrees with the left foot; in rapid succession leap/hop to a balanced position landing in a right-foot-left-foot succession.
10. Repeat step nine.
11. Repeat step eight.

PART FOUR: HOP-PUSH STEP

12. Unweight and turn 45 degrees to the right in the air.
13. As you land, push off the left foot and slide toward the right back corner.
14. Unweight and turn 45 degrees to the left in the air.
15. As you land, push off right foot and slide toward the left back corner.

Pros of Teaching Footwork: Puts the player in proper position to execute the desired skill.

Cons: Teaching the patterns correctly is difficult, and kids think it's boring to learn first.

What It Means to the Other Team: The other team will have to deal with an opponent who is more successful and efficient in skill execution.

How to Gauge a Player's Progress: Proper use of movement patterns in review and execution; proper use of movement patterns in drill situations; proper use of movement patterns in game situations.

Coaching Tip: A lot of kids have trouble learning the hop part of the foot patterns. It is either too small or nonexistent. Once the routine pattern has been acquired, emphasize the hop in review and execution.

SPIKE APPROACH STEPS

The person who spikes the ball must learn correct footwork to get in the most advantageous position to attack the ball. The height of the set and court position determines which foot pattern the spiker will use.

How They Work

Two-Step Approach: This is used for quick attacks where the sets are one foot above the net. From a standing position, the spiker leaps/hops forward, landing in rapid succession first with the foot of the striking arm and then with the opposite foot. From this base, the spiker jumps upward.

Three-Step Approach: This is used for medium-speed attacks. The spiker takes a normal step with the foot opposite the striking hand, then in rapid succession leaps forward with the foot of the striking hand and then the opposite foot. From this base, the spiker jumps upward.

Four-Step Approach: This is used for high-set attacks. The spiker takes a small step with the foot of the striking hand, then takes a bigger step with the foot opposite the striking hand, then leaps to the biggest step with the foot of the striking hand and rapidly plants with the opposite foot. From this base, the spiker jumps upward.

Backcourt Attack Approach: This is similar to the above approaches except that the spiker jumps upward and forward from behind the three-meter line and contacts the ball five to eight feet in front of the three-meter line.

Slide-Step Approach: This is a change of direction technique used to misdirect ("lose") the blocker. This is a four-step technique, with a pivot. The spiker (from the middle position) steps at the setter with the same foot as the striking hand, then takes a second step toward the setter with the opposite foot. The spiker then pivots and steps parallel to the net with the foot of the striking hand. The opposite foot takes a final step and leaps upward off one leg as the knee of the striking hand is lifted.

By learning all five of the spike-approach steps, players will be able to hit sets of different heights at various positions of the court.

BLOCKING FOOTWORK

There are two common footwork patterns used for blocking: the slide step and the crossover step. Since blocking should not be taught until the athletes are ready (when they're able to get their hands over the net), the footwork is included with general blocking techniques.

SERVING

The serve is the skill by which the ball is put into play from behind the end line. The ball must be tossed or released by the player and then struck with one hand. The basic objective of the serve is to start play by sending the ball into the opponent's court. Depending on the age and skill level of the player, the goal of the serve might change. An effective and consistent serve can disrupt the opponent's attacking system and on occasion score immediate points through aces.

Beginning players should be taught four basic serves: the side-float serve, the overhand-float serve, and eventually the jump serve and the jump-float serve.

THE SIDE-FLOAT SERVE

The side-float serve is ideal for young players who are ten years of age and under, because many younger children have not yet developed adequate shoulder and arm strength to effectively master the overhand techniques. They can quickly master the side-float serve and be ready to use it in games.

Pros of the Side-Float Serve: It is easy to learn and useful for all ages.

Cons: It gives the opponents more time to prepare to receive since it has to go up and over the net before coming down.

SIDE-FLOAT SERVE

Step 1: The hip joint of the leg opposite the striking hand is pointed at the desired target. The ball is placed on the pads of the fingers of the nonstriking hand and is held at chest height. A short step is taken with the foot opposite the striking hand as the striking arm and hand are pulled back just above knee height and the ball is released.

Step 2: The body weight is then transferred to the front foot, imparting a hip punch as the striking arm and hand swing forward. The contact is made with the base of the palm through the center of the ball. The striking hand follows through, finishing with the palm facing the top of the net.

What It Means to the Other Team: Since this serve is easy to execute, there is more pressure of having to return a consistent serve.

How to Gauge a Player's Progress: Success over the net.

Coaching Tip: The hip punch is critical to get power into the serve. Remind the server to move the hip forward with the arm before contact.

THE OVERHAND-FLOAT SERVE

This is the most basic serve. It is faster than the side-float serve and is very accurate if executed properly. The technique for this serve can be developed before the player has the strength to send the ball over the net from behind the end line. Youngsters can begin working on this serve from ten to fifteen feet from the net and, as their strength and control develops, gradually move back until they can eventually execute these serves from behind the end line.

OVERHAND-FLOAT SERVE

Step 1: Take a short step with the foot opposite the striking hand. The elbow of the striking hand is pulled back, opening the chest and shoulder. The arm opposite the striking hand is pushed up in front of the striking shoulder, allowing the ball to be released upward a few inches without any spin.

Step 2: The body weight is transferred to the front foot, imparting a hip punch as the striking shoulder and elbow rotate forward. The forearm of the striking arm swings forward horizontally, contacting the ball's center with the base of the palm of the striking hand following through the ball until the arm is extended forward at shoulder height, and the fingers are pointed upward.

Pros of the Overhand-Float Serve: The serve is usually very accurate and has a flat trajectory.

Cons: It may take longer for younger players to learn to execute the serve from the end line.

What It Means to the Other Team: There is pressure of having the weaker passers exploited since the serve is both accurate and fast.

How to Gauge a Player's Progress: Success over the net and to target areas.

Coaching Tip: Some players have problems with the toss, contact, and dropping their arm on the follow-through. The coach needs to watch the player's toss and be sure it is in front of the hitting shoulder. The contact is with the base of the palm, and the player keeps the arm up at shoulder level after the contact.

JUMP SERVE

Step 1: The jump serve begins by stepping forward with the foot opposite the tossing hand. Release the ball at chest height, tossing the ball with the fingers of the striking hand, imparting a forward spin on the ball.

Step 2: Leap to the ball with the same foot as the striking hand.

Step 3: Plant with the foot opposite the striking hand. Jump and lift both arms.

Step 4: Rotate the shoulder and elbow forward with the palm of the hand facing upward. Lead with the elbow and continue reaching upward for the ball with the forearm.

Step 5: Contact the bottom of the ball at its highest point with the base of the palm and with the elbow locked. Snap the wrist to a 90-degree angle to impart a top spin on the ball, and follow through.

THE JUMP SERVE

By far, the most exciting serve in the game is the jump serve. Every kid wants to learn it because it is similar to spiking. However, it is the most difficult serve to learn because of the complexity of the technique. If kids start closer to the net to learn the basics of the serve and move back to the end line gradually, they will eventually be successful.

Pros of the Jump Serve: This serve is the fastest and the most unpredictable.

Cons: There is a greater risk of error due to the complexity of the technique.

What It Means to the Other Team: Usually this serve catches the other team off guard and causes pressure of having to move quickly and play a ball moving at a fast pace.

How to Gauge a Player's Progress: Ability to consistently contact the ball in the air from behind the end line.

Coaching Tip: The toss is the major problem in this serve. The coach needs to watch the player's toss and make sure it is in front of the server and high enough to do the proper footwork. Also, the contact point is critical. If players hit the back of the ball, it will go out. If they hit the top of the ball, it will go into the net. They need to hit the bottom of the ball.

THE JUMP-FLOAT SERVE

This serve is a combination of the overhand-float serve and the jump serve. It is a little easier to teach, because the ball is tossed with both hands instead of one. The contact point is the same as the float serve, and the footwork is the same as the jump serve. It is a dynamic serve that is used in top programs.

The serve begins by stepping forward with the foot opposite the striking hand while lifting the ball with both hands to chest height with the elbows and wrists locked. The ball is released in front of the striking shoulder to about five feet above the head. The player then leaps to the ball with the same foot as the striking hand, plants with the foot opposite the striking hand, jumps and rotates the shoulder and the elbow forward. The contact is made in the center of the ball with the base of the palm of the hand and the follow-through is forward horizontally while punching through the ball. Keep the fingers pointed upward after contact. (See photo on page 45.)

Pros of the Jump-Float Serve: It's a faster alternative to the overhand float serve.

Cons: It takes a while to perfect the toss.

What It Means to the Other Team: It moves more than the float serve and is faster, so it is usually harder to pass.

How to Gauge a Player's Progress: Success over the net and to target areas.

Coaching Tip: The coach needs to watch the toss and the contact point and give feedback. Also, the player needs to stop the hand with the fingers upward after contact for consistency and direction.

FOREARM PASSING

Forearm passing is the method by which the serve is intercepted and rebounded off the forearms to the setter. The purpose of the pass is to deliver a serve to the setter in a position that allows the setter the option of setting a variety of spikers. The pass is considered the key to any team's offensive system. All volleyball players must acquire the forearm rebounding technique. When working with young children, it is recommended that a soft, light ball is used so it will not sting the arms on contact.

JUMP-FLOAT SERVE

Step 2: The ball is contacted on the fleshy part of the forearms, just above the wrists. The shoulders are shrugged and the elbows are locked.

FOREARM PASS

Step 1: Move behind the ball so it is positioned in front of the body between the knees. Feet are shoulder width apart, hips are under the ball, and the arms are extended in front of the body.

Step 3: The arms and the upper body serve as a stationary platform while the balls of the feet, ankles, and knees extend to do the actual passing.

Pros of the Forearm Pass: Consistent and accurate passing sets the foundation for effective offensive plays.

Cons: If a team does not have good passing technique, it becomes very easy for the opposing team to score a point.

What It Means to the Other Team: Strong passing and the ensuing offensive attack put maximum pressure on the defensive team's ability to stop the offensive play.

How to Gauge a Player's Progress: Increased accuracy in passing difficult serves shows improvement.

Coaching Tip: The two most common problems are players not moving to the ball and swinging their arms at the ball. Remind athletes to use the correct foot pattern (step-hop shown in step 1 on page 47), and to stop the arms on contact at chest level, never higher.

SETTING

The overhead pass is a skill executed above the head to direct the ball at the desired target. It is considered the most accurate skill in volleyball. Setting is the act of sending the pass to an attacker high enough so the ball can be played from above the net into the opponent's court. This is the most common use of the overhead pass. The person performing this skill is called a setter. The overhead pass is also used to receive a serve (instead of a forearm pass) to direct the pass to the setter, or it is used as a defensive technique or to send the ball over the net.

Pros of Setting: Setting allows for above-the-net contacts. Since the skill is so accurate, it is also the preferred skill to use on the first contact of a free ball.

Cons: This technique is difficult for young players to learn because it takes strong fingers and wrists to play the ball correctly. The forearm passing technique would be recommended to set the attackers if the players are not strong enough to use the overhand setting technique.

What It Means to the Other Team: There is more pressure to play a ball attacked from above the net.

How to Gauge a Player's Progress: Determine consistency of the set in terms of height and position along the net.

Coaching Tip: Setting consistency is dependent on accurate service reception. Have athletes practice setting off a pass instead of a toss.

SETTING

Step 1: When executing a set, the person moves quickly to the ball and does a hop/step to a balanced position with the right shoulder to the net and the right foot forward. The ball is contacted on the finger pads in a position above the forehead.

Step 2: As soon as the ball touches the hands, the ankles, knees, and elbows extend up and through the ball, and the weight is transferred from the front foot up onto the toes. The wrists are rotated so the fingers point to the high point of the flight of the ball.

PUSH PASS

Described on page 48.

SETTING VARIATIONS: THE BACK SET AND THE QUICK SET

The back set adds deception to the attacks. The starting point of the technique is similar to the front set, but as the ankles and knees extend up, the upper back arches, the elbows move up and back to the ears, and the eyes follow the ball as it is released backward and over the forehead. The defending team must react more quickly and be prepared to play balls coming from both sides of the court.

The quick set adds speed and deception to the attack. In executing a quick set, the wrists remain cocked, the elbows move slowly upward, and the ball is directed to a height of two balls above the net (approximately one foot). The attacker jumps as the setter contacts the ball. The defending team has less time to react due to the speed of the attack.

PUSH PASS

This technique is similar to setting but is used on service receive or defense to direct the ball at the setter. The hands are open and fingers and wrists are stiff. As the ball contacts the hands, the wrists and fingers remain still, and the forearms push the ball to the setter.

SPIKING

Spiking (hitting) is the most visible skill in volleyball, and the one skill every kid wants to learn. The spike is the technique used to send the ball into the opponent's court at maximum speed, incorporating a full swinging arm motion above the head. The purpose of the spike is to send the ball to an undefended position on the opponent's court or to a defender who cannot control the dig. Spiking is fun, but it is a difficult skill to master and teach. It requires a combination of timing, balance, strength, and quickness. Without proper mechanics, spiking can be frustrating if the ball continues to go out of bounds or into the net. A basic rule of thumb for teaching spiking to kids is to start deep (approximately fifteen feet from the net) and gradually work closer to the net as spiking is mastered. Proper arm swing needs to be taught along with four spiking approaches discussed on pages 38 and 39.

THE SPIKING ARM SWING

This can be practiced without the ball and footwork.

1. Draw both arms back behind the body to a 90-degree angle with the elbows locked.

2. Bring both arms forward until they are pointing to the ground and parallel with the legs.

3. Begin to draw the elbow of the striking arm up and backward with the wrist and hand of the striking arm relaxed and pointing down as the nonstriking arm continues upward until the nonstriking arm is pointing at the ball.

4. Pull the nonstriking hand and elbow forward and down, elevating the striking shoulder, and reach up and forward with the striking elbow.

5. Reach up with the forearm of the striking arm while bending the elbow of the non-striking arm and pulling up the hand of the nonstriking arm.

6. Contact the bottom third of the ball at the base of the palm of the striking hand and rotate the wrist over the ball so that the hand is at a 90-degree angle with the arm and the fingers pointing down.

When teaching the arm swing, have the players stand and move their arms into the correct position when you say the numbers (one through six). Make corrections as needed.

Once the footwork and arm swing have been taught, the final skill should look like the photos on pages 50 and 51.

Pros of the Spike: Spiking efficiency can increase your probability of winning rallies, which means more points for your team.

Cons: Players are likely to make mistakes if they don't learn the value of consistency. Some players try to hit every ball as hard as they can instead of keeping it in the court.

What It Means to the Other Team: A high-speed spike is difficult for the opponents to dig.

How to Gauge a Player's Progress: Look for success in each of these progressions:

1. Observe the arm swing with the ball (standing).
2. Observe the approach and jump, and incorporate the arm swing without the ball.
3. Observe the approach and jump, and incorporate the arm swing with the ball.

Coaching Tip: Hitting the ball into the net or out of bounds is an immediate point for the other team. Remind players to contact the bottom third of the ball with the base of the palm, hit up, and then snap the wrist over the ball.

SPIKING

Step 1: When spiking the ball, the approach begins as the ball nears the height of its trajectory. The first step is taken with the foot opposite the striking hand, and the arms are in a position to begin swinging backward.

Step 2: The second step is a longer step. On this step, the heel is planted to slow forward momentum and the arms are drawn back to an angle of 90 degrees behind the body.

Step 3: On the last step, the arms have swung forward and up, and the foot opposite the striking arm is turned in at a 45-degree angle to stop forward momentum.

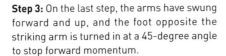

Step 4: As the legs and ankles extend and push the body off the ground, the nonstriking arm is lifted up and pointed at the ball while the elbow of the striking arm is pulled back with the hand relaxed and the fingers pointed downward. The shoulder and elbow of the striking arm then rotate forward, the elbow leads up and the palm points upward.

Step 5: The shoulder reaches and the forearm extends, locking the elbow. The bottom third of the ball is contacted with the base of the palm in front of the striking shoulder.

Step 6: The striking hand is then rotated up and over the ball and the wrist extends down at a 90-degree angle. The landing should be cushioned by bending the knees to absorb the shock.

THE TIP

The tip is an offspeed attack in which the attacker places the ball behind or around the block. The purpose is to fool the opponent into thinking that a hard-driven spike is coming and then catch them off guard with a soft shot.

Pros of the Tip: The correct placement of a tip can throw off an opposing team's defense.

Cons: If an opposing team covers the tip, it is easy to dig.

What It Means to the Other Team: They must be ready for anything and learn to move and play a balanced defense.

How to Gauge a Player's Success: He is able to tip right, left, center, and over a block.

Coaching Tip: Make sure your players don't make a weak approach when they tip. It should look like they are going to spike until the contact.

THE DIG

The dig is the basic skill used to receive the opponent's attack. The purpose is to control the hard-driven spike from the opposing team and initiate a counterattack. The primary skill involved is the two-hand dig. Players of all ages must be taught and drilled in proper defensive technique. Some of the most exciting plays in volleyball are initiated with a good dig.

Pros of the Dig: Accurate digging is an exciting technique that can set your team up for a strong offensive play and ignite their momentum.

Cons: Beginning players may find the ball hurts their arms.

What It Means to the Other Team: A successful dig thwarts the attacking team and forces it to quickly adjust from offense to defense.

How to Gauge a Player's Progress: The accuracy of the dig determines progress. The ball should be dug five to ten feet from the net to the center of the court.

Coaching Tip: Some players are afraid of being hurt by the ball. Also, some players tend to swing at the ball instead of absorbing the force of the contact. Coaches can let air out of the balls to reduce the sting on the players' arms when they practice digging. Coaches can also control the speed and pace of the ball during digging drills by hitting the ball with less power for the beginning players.

THE TIP

The approach and arm swing are identical to the spike. The difference is that the contact on the ball is on the finger pads instead of the base of the palm.

Step 2: The ball is played inside of the knees with two hands. The digging motion is a scooping motion in which the top of the thumbs are scooped under the ball, rebounding the ball off the top of the wrists. The scooping motion undercuts the ball, which imparts a back spin on it. Control and accuracy are gained by merely pointing the thumbs at the intended target.

THE DIG

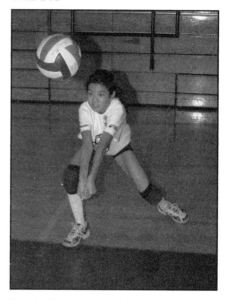

Step 1: The feet are at least shoulder width apart with the weight forward and the arms in front of the body. The defender steps at the ball, getting the hips lower than the ball.

04

THE LATERAL STEP AND SCOOP

Another digging technique is used when the ball is outside of body line. The defender must step laterally, keeping the ball inside the knee, and drop the inside shoulder using the digging and scooping motions described in the step two photo on page 53.

THE SPRAWL AND THE ROLL

These are emergency defensive techniques used to extend the playing range of the defender or to recover after retrieving a ball out of normal playing range. The athlete must be able to go to the floor and execute these skills to the left and the right. These skills are actually easier for younger athletes to learn because they are closer to the floor and don't have as far to fall.

THE SPRAWL

This is the fundamental technique used when the athlete must reach completely forward and extend parallel to the floor. It allows the player to go to the floor safely and get up quickly.

THE SPRAWL

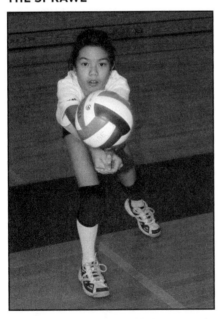

Step 1: Step through to a 90-degree angle. Undercut and scoop the ball to the intended target, preferably with both hands.

Step 2: Turn the lead knee outward and place the hand opposite the lead knee on the floor. Reach forward over the lead leg. Place your body on the floor.

THE ROLL

This technique is used to contact a low ball out of the body line. The athlete rolls over after the contact to get up quicker. This is a safe technique since the athlete does not roll over either the shoulder or the neck, and it provides extension of the body to the ball. (See pages 56 and 57.)

Pros of the Sprawl and the Roll: These two techniques will increase the range of motion of the athletes when playing defense.

Cons: These techniques must be taught properly or there is risk for injury.

What It Means to the Other Team: Mastering and successfully using floor moves makes it more difficult for the attacking team to put the ball on the floor.

How to Gauge a Player's Progress: Ability to execute the move, first without the ball. Then, when the moves have been mastered, start with slow tosses of the ball and check for mastery before increasing the speed of the ball.

Coaching Tips: Some kids contact the floor too hard because they forget to go to the floor from a low position; some are fearful of learning these moves because they are afraid to get hurt. Use a padded mat, thick rug, lawn, or sand to practice and learn these floor moves. This will help to remove the fear factor.

BLOCKING

The block is a skill that incorporates jumping at the net and holding the arms above the head to stop or slow down the opponent's attack or channel the ball to the defenders. Since this technique must be executed above the net to be effective, it is not recommended that young athletes use this technique in a game until they are able to seal off areas of the court. Players seal off areas of the court by the placement of their hands above the net. Proper hand placement should prevent the opposing spikers from sending the ball into certain areas of the court.

Though blocking should not be used in game situations until it serves a positive function for the team defense, all athletes should be taught to block at a lowered net or a rope strung at a proper height so they develop correct footwork and blocking technique, which can be used later when their height and jumping ability allows them to contribute their blocking to the team defense.

THE ROLL

04

Step 1: In preparation for the roll, step to a 90-degree angle. Undercut and scoop the ball to the target, preferably with both hands.

Step 2: Turn the lead knee inward and place the hand opposite the lead knee on the floor. Reach forward with the arm over the lead leg and place the side of your body on the floor.

Step 3: Roll over the back and onto the stomach.

Step 4: Push off the balls of the feet and the hands.

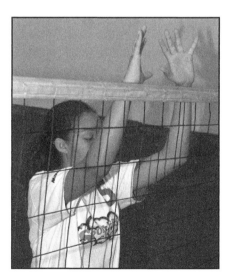

Step 5: Get up.

THE BLOCK

Step 1: In the ready position, knees are slightly bent, feet are shoulder width apart, body is close to net with shoulders parallel to net, and hands are at shoulder height.

Step 2: Knees and elbows begin to extend as the feet and ankles push off the ground. The elbows are raised higher in front of the eyes with the forearms parallel to the net.

Step 3: As the attacker's elbow moves forward, the blocker presses upward and forward until elbows lock. Contact is made on muscles at the base of the thumbs. Fingers are spread, and hands and fingers are rigid.

57

BLOCKING FOOT PATTERNS

To correctly position oneself to block, it is essential to master two fundamental movement patterns. They are the slide-step and the crossover-step patterns.

Slide Step (Step, Close, Step)

This pattern is used when the block must move a distance of up to five feet. It is used by outside blockers and by middle blockers adjusting to quick sets. (It is also used to get into position to pass and dig without step four.)

1. Step with the near/lead foot in the intended direction.
2. The other foot closes to the first step.
3. The near/lead foot takes a second step to provide balance.
4. With the feet under the corresponding shoulders, jump to block.

Crossover Step

This pattern is employed when the blocker must move from five to fifteen feet. It is primarily used by middle blockers to move into position to block outside sets (sets that are close to the sidelines). (See page 59 for step-by-step instructions.)

Pros of the Block: Blocking adds a challenge to the opposing offense, because they must hit around the block or use it (the attacker hits the ball off the hands of the blocker and it goes out of bounds).

Cons: If the blockers have poor technique, they can make errors such as touching the net or being used by the attacker. There is a greater risk for injury since the players are jumping at the net within close proximity to each other.

What It Means to the Other Team: Proper movement and positioning allows for a better block, which makes it more difficult for the opponent to initiate a successful attack.

How to Gauge a Player's Progress: Make sure the athlete can block straight ahead and penetrate over the net before moving the hands to the sides.

Coaching Tip: Jumping sideways and not penetrating into the opponent's court are two major problems with blocking. The coach needs to emphasize proper movement and planting before the jump is executed, and extending the arms up and forward on contact. Also, pushing off the back leg when initiating the first step of both blocking moves will provide more explosiveness and quicker movement.

THE CROSSOVER

Step 1: Turn the near/lead foot toward the intended sideline and step in that direction by pushing off the back foot.

Step 2: Leap toward the intended sideline with the other foot, air pivoting so that upon landing, the foot that took the second step is pointed at the net.

Step 3: Plant the near/end foot at the net on the final step to provide balance.

Step 4: With both feet under the corresponding shoulder, jump to block.

THE REBOUND

Hand Position: One hand is placed behind the other with thumbs interlocked. The wrists are cocked backward. (Note the position of the thumbs.)

Step 1: Move to the ball so it is positioned directly above the forehead. Bend the knees.

Step 2: Contact the ball at the base of the palms. Extend the elbows forward and upward.

04

REBOUND

The rebound is a defensive technique using an open-hand dig to retrieve a high ball hit by the opponent. Even though the push pass can also be used, this skill allows more stability for the younger player since the hands are interlocked. It is more effective in defending a high, hard-driven spike.

Pros of the Rebound: It's a great defensive technique for the younger athlete to get the ball to the target by using the body and the hands.

Cons: It has been replaced by the push pass at higher levels as the hands get stronger.

What It Means to the Other Team: It becomes more challenging for the opponent to hit a ball deep in the court.

How to Gauge a Player's Progress: The ball should be dug five to ten feet from the net in the center of the court.

Coaching Tip: Coaches can control the speed and pace of the ball during rebound drills by hitting the ball with less power to the beginner players.

CONTACT POINTS FOR THE BASIC SKILLS

All of the basic skills have a contact point that is most advantageous for accuracy. The contact point is where the ball actually hits the arms or the hands during a particular skill. In the pictures on pages 62–64, the contact points for the basic skills are indicated in black.

FINAL THOUGHTS

The keys to teaching fundamentals are repetition and feedback. The athletes should have many opportunities to try each skill, and the coach or teacher needs to be observant in giving correct feedback. Chapter eight has several drills and a practice plan to incorporate skill training into your practices.

Instead of focusing on mistakes (and there will be a lot), focus on what the kids are doing right and reward them with praise. You want to have your athletes become "unconscious competents" when it comes to executing fundamentals. They should eventually be able to do these skills without even thinking about them. If they can get to this level, they will be able to enjoy the game to the fullest, and your job as a coach or teacher will become a lot easier.

SIDE-FLOAT SERVE

OVERHAND-FLOAT SERVE

The contact point for all serves is at the base of the palm.

FOREARM PASS

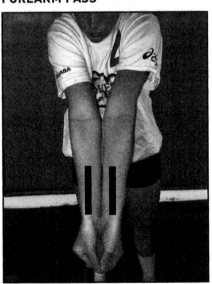

The contact point is on the forearms, just above the wrists. The base of the thumbs are turned out, and the outsides of the palms are pressed together. The fingers of one hand are placed on the fingers of the other. The thumbs are locked on the first joint of the middle finger and pointed downward.

SETTING AND THE PUSH PASS

The ball contacts the pads of the fingers. The hand position is above the forehead. The hands are cupped, fingers spread, and the thumbs are pointed toward each other.

SPIKING

The bottom third of the ball is contacted with the base of the palm.

DIGGING

The contact of the ball is made on the top of the thumbs, which scoop under the ball, rebounding it off the wrists, and creating a back spin on the ball. The thumbs point at the intended target.

04

BLOCKING

The contact is made on the muscle at the base of the thumbs, forming an inverted "V." Fingers are spread, and hands and fingers are rigid.

COURT POSITIONS AND RESPONSIBILITIES

05

There are six basic positions on a six-person volleyball team. They are the setter, middle blocker, outside hitter (sometimes called a swing hitter), opposite hitter (the person opposite the setter), libero, and defensive specialist. These positions can be condensed to two setters, two middle blockers, and two outside hitters or expanded to one setter, one opposite hitter, two middle blockers, two swing hitters, one libero, and one or more defensive specialists, depending on team personnel. Each position has its particular demands and responsibilities. When kids are first learning the game, they should be taught all the skills and be allowed to try all the positions. As they become more proficient, certain attributes will stand out, which will enable them to be more successful at a specialized position. Since volleyball players must rotate after each side out, they still have to be well-rounded players and have basic skills. However, certain skills will be emphasized more than others depending on the demands of the position.

THE SETTER

A setter is very much like a quarterback in football. She is responsible for running the offense. She must put up good sets for the attackers and make good choices depending on her hitters and the other team's defense. If she is setting a 5-1 offense, which incorporates five hitters and one setter, she sets in every rotation. Obviously, she must love to set. If she is setting in a 6-2 offense, which incorporates six hitters and two setters, she sets when she is in the back row and becomes an attacker when she is in the front row. In a 4-2 system, she sets in the front row, and passes in the back row. She does not hit, unless she wants to attack the pass, while in the front row or hit from behind the attack line while in the back row.

The setter calls the receive or passing formations (see chapter six), sets the offense and transition, plays defense, serves, and usually blocks and hits from the right-front position. To be an effective setter, an athlete must have these five qualifications:

1. The player must be quick to the ball. This is important to give the setter time to read the defense and make the appropriate setting choices. If the setter is late, there is usually only one option. If the hitters are calling their sets, it gives them time to get into position. A setter who beats the ball to position will always make an offense more stable and smooth.

2. The player must have strong hands and good setting technique. A setter must be able to set the ball from anywhere on the court to the hitters. This means setters must have strong hands and a solid release. She must set from the same basic hand position (above the forehead) to keep the blockers on the other team guessing where the set is going to go. Referees will call a lift or a double hit on a mishandled set, which will end up being an immediate point for the opponent. Obviously, most teams can't afford to have the other team get points on setting errors, so your setter must be fundamentally sound and still be able to set most passes with the overhead-setting technique.

3. The player must be smart. A setter makes choices on each pass about where to set the ball and to whom. He must know his hitters, understand their tendencies, and know who to set when it's crunch time. He also needs to know how to read the defense and when to dump the ball (send it over to the opponents on the second contact). A smart setter always makes the hitters look good. He must know when to set a quicker set and when to go with a higher, slower set. He is responsible for getting the team into offensive rhythm.

4. The player must be unselfish. Even though the setter controls the offense, most of the credit usually goes to the hitters. They are the ones who get the kills, which usually get the attention of the spectators. A setter needs to understand this and be willing to accept it as part of the game. The hitters always appreciate a good setter. Coaches must be sure to give credit to the setter if she is doing a good job. A setter must be giving and not expect to receive much attention.

5. The player must be a good leader. Since a setter controls the offense, he is the leader on the court. He must be able to handle pressure and help the team when they are in trouble. He must be emotionally stable and be able to calm a team down when the pressure is on. An emotionally unstable setter will sabotage the team in pressure situations by distracting the team and forcing them to doubt themselves. A setter who is a good leader will get the team to focus in important situations.

As a coach, you must choose your setters wisely. Your team's success and your sanity depend on it.

THE MIDDLE BLOCKER

The middle blocker, who is responsible for putting up a solid, consistent block in the middle, must be able to move to the outside blocker to form a double block and must be an aggressive attacker, especially from the middle of the net. If your team is not ready to block yet, choose players who will have the most potential to play this position in the future and start teaching them blocking footwork and how to attack out of the middle consistently. When they are in the back row, they should be efficient at passing, defense, and serving and should ideally be able to attack from the back row. If they are not strong back-row players, they can be replaced by the libero or defensive specialists who play the back position, or a service receive pattern can be called in which they do not have passing responsibilities (see chapter six).

There are four qualifications an athlete must have to be an effective middle blocker:

1. The player must be able to play above the net and must have a great jump, be tall, or both. Ideally, a middle blocker should be able to get her elbows above the net (every coach's dream!). The reason a middle blocker needs to be so far above the net is to take away the opponent's hitting angles. The more a middle blocker can take away from the opponent's offense, the easier it is for the rest of your team to play defense.

2. The player must have quick movements. A middle blocker has to move quickly forward and back to hit the quick sets, or fake the quicks and immediately be ready to block the opposing hitters. Quick lateral movement is imperative to put up a double block with the outside blockers and in an advanced offensive system; they must be able to hit a slide. A middle blocker does a lot of quick explosive moves, sometimes without contacting the ball. This should not deter the middle blocker from staying aggressive and continuing to go in for the set.

3. The player must be aggressive. I like to think of this position as the Terminator. He should love to block and put the ball away. This is not a position for a timid player. An aggressive middle blocker can shut down another team's offense on pure determination and desire. He usually makes the big blocks or hits the quick sets that can turn around a game's momentum. Off the court, a middle blocker can be the nicest kid in the world. On the court, he must be fierce.

4. The player must have good body control, which is not only important for efficiency but also for injury prevention. A middle blocker must be able to jump straight up from a forward and side approach. If a middle blocker cannot control her body, she can

67

injure herself, her teammates, and the other team. Good footwork is imperative for a middle blocker.

THE OUTSIDE HITTER

The outside hitter is the workhorse on the team. He must be able to hit from anywhere on the court and be consistent. He usually gets the highest percentage of the sets, so your team's success will most likely depend on his hitting efficiency. He also does the majority of the passing. In the back row, he usually plays the left-back defensive position that digs a high percentage of balls. He must also be able to attack out of the back row as efficiently as he can attack from the front row if you are running a full-court attack.

There are five qualifications a player must possess to be a good outside hitter:

1. The player must have good fundamental skills. An outside hitter must be able to do every skill with a high level of consistency. She should ideally be great at passing, defense, and spiking and be able to block when she is in the front row. The outside hitter is the stabilizer on the team.

2. The player must be in great shape. He will get the majority of the sets and have to pass a majority of the balls. He will also be in defensive positions to which most of the balls will be hit. He must have great anaerobic and aerobic capacity and be able to continue to be consistent during a long match. An outside hitter needs to be energetic and keep going and going. The team cannot afford for him to get tired.

3. The player must be able to handle pressure and want the ball. Since the outside hitter passes, hits, and digs a majority of the balls, she must want the ball to come to her, especially in pressure situations. The person who plays "dodgeball" and does not want to be set unless it is perfect does not belong in this position. A great outside hitter wants the ball when it is the toughest. She wants to be served, she wants the set, and she will give it her best effort every time without backing off. She can also recover quickly from a mistake and is always ready for the next play.

4. The player must be smart. An outside hitter must know how and when to hit to different areas of the court. He must also know which sets he can hit and which he needs to keep in the court. He must also develop a sense about when to tip the ball. This player must study the defense and be able to react to it with smart hitting choices.

5. The player must be able to concentrate. All players need to be able to concentrate, but this player has to be a rock. Since she contacts the ball so often, it's important the outside hitter does not get thrown off by distractions. If your outside hitter loses her concentration, usually the rest of the team follows.

THE OPPOSITE HITTER (RIGHT-SIDE HITTER)

This position plays opposite a 5-1 setter, or front row for a 6-2 setter who only sets when in the back row. This position can end up being one of the most important. The opposite hitter must block the opposing team's outside hitters and be ready to hit or set the transition if the setter digs the ball. In the 5-1 system, this person plays back row, serves, helps with passing, is a good backcourt attacker, and usually plays defense behind the front-row setter. Even though this position does not have the movement demands the previous positions require, very often it is this player who will make the key plays that can make the difference between winning and losing.

A player in this position must have these three important qualities:

1. The player must be able to play above the net. As with the middle blocker, the opposite hitter must be able to take away the opposing hitter's angles by putting up a strong, solid block. He must have a good jump and get as high above the net as possible. If you have a tall player who can get above the net but does not move well laterally, this might be a good position for him to try. For young teams that are not ready to block, the opposite hitter should be able to set and hit from the right side.

2. The player should have good setting technique. When the setter digs the ball, the opposite hitter will set the dig to the hitters. She should be able to push the ball to the outside hitter and be competent at setting the middle as well.

3. The player needs to be alert. Since the opposite hitter is on the right side of the court, he does not get as many sets as a left-side hitter because it is more difficult to back set. The opposite hitter must stay alert, expect the set at all times, and be ready to hit. In some offenses, the opposite hitter can swing to the middle position, which will give him more hitting opportunities.

It should be noted that, in this position and in the setting position, there is an advantage if the player is left-handed. That puts her on hand, which means the ball does not have to cross her face before she hits it. With left-handed setters in the front row, it is easier for her to catch the defense off guard with hits over on the second contact.

THE LIBERO

This position is for the "ball control specialist." This player is designated by wearing a different color uniform from the rest of the team and is allowed to replace any player in the back row without it counting as a substitution. There is no limit to the number of libero replacements, and they do not count against team substitutions. The libero can go in for anyone in the back row but may not attack the ball from above the height of the net or handset the ball from in front of the attack line. Usually, the libero is not allowed to serve, but the NCAA allows it so this rule may change soon to allow the libero to serve at more levels. When leaving the game, the libero must remain on the bench for one play before re-entering the game for a back-row player. This player must possess outstanding ball-control skills first and foremost, great passing skills, and pinpoint digging skills. The libero is in the game most of the time.

This position allows for more flexibility in substitutions, and, if used properly, will improve a team's ball control. We have seen average teams become great when they have an awesome libero. They rule the back court. Height is not a limitation for this position.

A great libero must meet these specifications:

1. The player must be quick. Liberos are usually the quickest players on the court.

2. The player must be willing to go to the floor and make the big defensive plays. This is her primary job and role on the team.

3. The player must have pinpoint passing and digging skills. These skills help set the team's rhythm.

4. The player must be willing to take more court to compensate for a weaker passer or digger. If the ball is between the libero and another player, the libero must be aggressive and take it.

5. Since she is on the court most of the time, the libero must be a leader. She directs the other players as to where to go on serve receive and defense.

THE DEFENSIVE SPECIALIST

A defensive specialist also only plays the backcourt position, but he does not play as much as the libero since his substitutions count. He can only enter the game three times. The player must have good passing skills, be able to serve under pressure, and play exceptional defense. He must be able to go to the floor to play a ball. He must also be able to hit out of the back row. A defensive specialist is often the heart and soul of the team. He is usually the most unselfish person on the team, and when he comes into the game can act as a spark plug and turn a game around. Also, if he does a great job, he could find himself playing the libero position, especially if the assigned libero is not doing her job. For a player to be great defensive specialist must meet these qualifications:

1. The player must be quick. There is no such thing as a slow defensive specialist. He must be quick with both his movements and his decisions.

2. The player must be willing to sacrifice her body—not that she should try to hurt herself, but she should be willing to go to the floor and make the big defensive plays that can win the game. There is no such thing as an undiggable ball to a defensive specialist.

3. The player must be mentally tough. Since he is not in the game the whole time, he must be ready to go into the game in any situation. It is very demanding to come off the bench and into the game when the match is close or on the line. He must be able to handle pressure.

4. The player must have good passing skills. Most of the time, that is why she is in the game.

5. The player must be unselfish. I believe all teams and leagues should consider this position just as valuable as any other since it is so demanding. However, the reality of the situation is that, most of the time, this player gets very little of the credit or glory. Therefore, he must be willing to accept this as a reality and still contribute to the team. The coach and the other teammates, however, do need to reinforce him and give him credit and attention when he is doing a good job. Otherwise, he might lose heart, and your team will suffer as a result.

All positions have their specifications and demands. When working with young children, they should all get to set, hit, pass, and serve. It really is not necessary to designate assigned positions until they start to block or if you have some kids who are much further along than others in skills such as setting. As kids start to develop, certain traits will become discernable, and you can begin working them into certain positions where they and the team can have the most success. This takes time, and kids should be able to try different positions before they find the one best suited for them. Experiment and observe. Don't lock kids into a position that will restrict their development as players. Give them time and opportunities. Everyone has a role in this game.

05

06

Offense in volleyball comes into play when the other team is serving. In this situation, you are trying to prevent the other team from getting points. When you select either a service receive pattern (how the players position on the court to receive a serve) or an offensive system (which determines the setter's starting point and how many players can attack the ball), you need to be aware of the strategies of the various patterns and systems and have a realistic evaluation of your team's strengths and weaknesses.

Since the scoring system has changed to rally, it is important that your team is efficient at whatever offensive strategy is used and does not make unforced errors, which include passing, setting, or hitting errors, or a ball dropping between players. Winning at most levels is determined by which team makes the least errors. If you can convince your team that what they do is more important than what the other team does, they will concentrate on their skills and have a greater chance for success.

OFFENSE

Training your team to attack at the top levels sometimes involves running a quick set to the middle hitter.

HOW TO SET UP A SERVICE RECEIVE PATTERN

Since passing accuracy is paramount to the success of the offense, you need to put your team in the most advantageous positions of the court to pass the ball accurately to the target area for the setter to run the attack. Your team needs to be confident in each rotation so they can prevent the opposing team from getting points and get the ball back so they can serve. A coach also needs to be aware of potential player overlaps at the moment of service. See chapter one for the overlap rule and examples. Here are four service receive patterns used in volleyball:

For consistency of illustration, the following receive patterns show the setter in the middle-front position. However, the setter could be in any other position on the court, depending on rotation and offensive system used.

THE FIVE-PERSON RECEIVE PATTERN: THE W FORMATION

A very good receive pattern used for youth volleyball is the five-person receive. In this pattern, the players do not have to cover as much ground to pass the ball. A volleyball court seems big to young, small players. In this receive pattern, five people are in position to pass the ball to the target area, which is between the middle-front and the right-front positions about five feet off the net (the perfect pass). The five passers line up on the court like the letter *W*, with two players deep on the court, two players short, and one player in the middle just behind the attack line. The two deep players are responsible for passing the deep serves, and the three front players pass the shorter serves. If the ball is served between players, the one who is moving toward the target area has priority and will pass the ball (or so the coach hopes).

FIVE-PERSON RECEIVE PATTERN

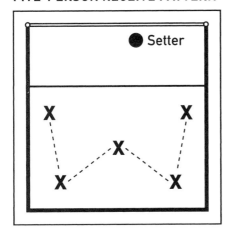

There are five passers in this receive pattern, which is sometimes called the "W-service reception." The setter does not pass, but rather moves to the intended target when the ball is served.

The setter can be in the front or back row when the ball is served, depending on which offensive system is used, and releases to the target area where the ball will ideally be passed after the serve is contacted. This receive pattern can be moved up closer to the net or deeper to the end line depending on where the opposing team is serving.

Since there are five potential passers in this formation, communication is vital so players will not run into each other and the ball will not drop between players. You must teach your players to call the ball and communicate with each other. "Mine," "yours," "in" and "out" should be communicated immediately and consistently on every service reception. On a deep serve, the front-row players should open their lanes (turn sideways to the back-row players) to give the back-row passers a better view of the ball.

ADVANTAGES
1. There are few holes for the opposing team to attack on the serve.
2. There are more passing opportunities for all your players than the other receive patterns.
3. The potential of overlaps is minimal.
4. This receive pattern works well for a 4-2, 5-1, or 6-2 offensive system.

DISADVANTAGES
1. A weak passer can be exploited by a good serving team.
2. The middle hitters may have trouble getting to their attack positions if they are hitting a quick set in the middle (see chapter one for the definition of a quick set).

THE FOUR-PERSON RECEIVE PATTERN

This receive pattern involves four potential passers in the receive pattern. The two players not involved in the service receive are the setter and one other player. The positions of the players on the court resemble a *U*. There is more court for each of the players to cover in order to pass the ball. For this reason, this pattern is usually not recommended for younger teams.

ADVANTAGES
1. It gives the middle hitter more time to position for the middle attack.
2. If a player is not passing well, this pattern can be used as an adjustment to eliminate that player from the receive pattern.

DISADVANTAGE
1. There is a big hole for the opponents to attack with the serve in the center front of the court.

FOUR-PERSON RECEIVE PATTERN

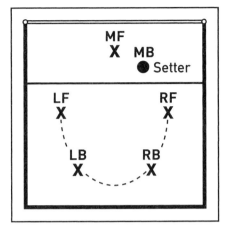

Four players pass all the serves. The remaining two players are not involved in passing.

THREE-PERSON RECEIVE PATTERN

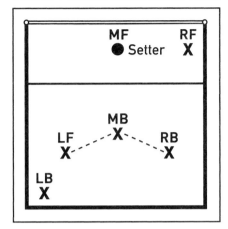

In this pattern, three players pass all the serves. The other three players are not involved in passing.

THE THREE-PERSON RECEIVE PATTERN

Some teams are very successful in running a five-person or four-person receive pattern. Other teams get into trouble because of poor passers who become serving targets for the other team, or because the four-person receive pattern creates a big hole in the middle that can be exploited by a good serving team. The three-person receive pattern can solve these problems and is becoming more popular at the high school and college levels. It can be taught at the youth level as well. In this pattern, three passers are responsible to cover the whole court on service receive. Usually one person is on the end line (out of the receive pattern) and another is at the net. The setter comes in as usual to the target area. The three people who are passing should obviously be your best passers and be able to move to the ball quickly.

ADVANTAGES
1. There are no holes for the opposing team to exploit.
2. You can get your poor passers out of the receive pattern.
3. You can get your middle hitters into position faster.

DISADVANTAGES
1. Each of the three passers has to cover a lot more court than in the five- or four-person receive patterns.

2. The overlap potential is very high. Players need to be aware of their court positions before the ball is served.

THE TWO-PERSON RECEIVE PATTERN

This receive pattern uses only two people to pass the serves. This pattern can only be used if you have two people who can move quickly to the ball and have excellent passing technique. This pattern will not work well with marginal passers. I remember seeing one high school team run this receive pattern with two passers who were slow and inaccurate. Obviously, they didn't win many games.

Passers must cover the whole court on receiving a serve just like a doubles team would on the beach. Court responsibilities are cut in half.

ADVANTAGES
1. There is no confusion about who is responsible for passing the ball.
2. The passers tend to get into a rhythm from passing so often.
3. The weaker passers do not have to worry about receiving the serve. Instead, they can get ready to hit (which is probably what they want to do the most anyway).

DISADVANTAGES
1. The short serve is harder to receive with only two people in the pattern.
2. The passers are often at a disadvantage to get into their hitting positions if they are passing all the time. Their hitting rhythm can get off.
3. The overlap potential is very high.

TWO-PERSON RECEIVE PATTERN

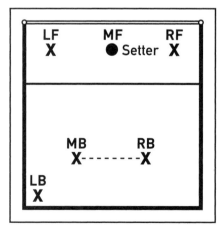

Here two players pass all the serves while the other four players are not involved in passing.

OFFENSIVE SYSTEMS

Once you have decided which receive pattern(s) work best for your team, it is time for you to decide which offensive system you will run. The main objective of any system is to gain a strategic advantage by getting the setter to the target area of the court to execute an attack. Some systems use a front-row setter, while others use a back-row setter, and some use combinations of front- and back-row setters. There are two innovative systems that work well in youth volleyball: the 6-6 and the 6-3. However, the three most common systems used in youth volleyball are the 4-2, the 6-2 and the 5-1.

THE 4-2 OFFENSIVE SYSTEM (FRONT-ROW SETTER SYSTEM)

In a 4-2 system, there are two setters on the court and four hitters. The setters are placed opposite each other in the rotational order, so when one is in the front row, the other setter is in the back row. The setters set in the positions across the front row (left front, middle front, and right front). When they rotate to the back row, they become passers.

ADVANTAGES
1. It is very easy for the setters to get to the target area, since they do not have to move very far. (The target area is the area that allows the setter the option of setting a variety of spikes. Usually this is five feet from the net, in the center of the court or slightly to the right.)
2. The overlap potential is very low.
3. Also, the setter can hit the pass in a surprise attackinstead of setting the ball.

DISADVANTAGES
1. Since the setter sets while in the front-row position, there will only be two attackers in the front row at a time.
2. Setters realize they will never get to hit and might not want to stay at this position for very long.

THE 6-2 OFFENSIVE SYSTEM (BACK-ROW SETTER SYSTEM)

In a 6-2 offense, there are two setters on the court who are opposite each other in the rotational order (similar to the 4-2). However, they set when they are in the back-row positions and become hitters when they are in the front row. This is how you end up with six hitters and two setters (6-2). To run this offense, you need to have six players who can function as spikers and two of those spikers who can also

THE 4-2 OFFENSE

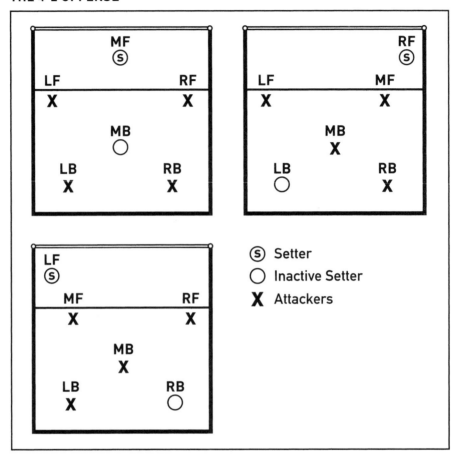

The 4-2 offensive system uses four attackers and two setters. A five-person receive pattern works best with this system, although the other receive patterns could also be utilized. One setter is always in the front row. When the front setter rotates to the back row, the person who was opposite in the lineup becomes the new front-row setter.

function as setters. The setters must be quicker than in the 4-2 system since they must cover more ground to get to the target area to set the attack because they are coming from the back row.

ADVANTAGES

1. You can run three attackers at the net instead of two, which is more of an offensive threat to the opposing team.

78

THE 6-2 OFFENSE

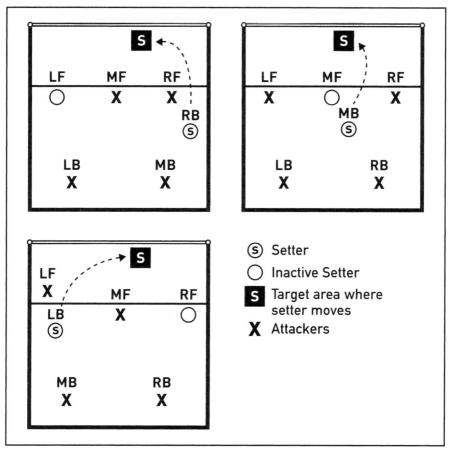

The 6-2 offensive system uses six attackers and two setters. In this system, the setter comes from the back row to set. When the back-row setter rotates to the front row, he becomes a hitter, while the new back-row setter sets the next three rotations.

2. Setters become hitters when they rotate to the front row, and they usually like the opportunity to hit as well as set.

DISADVANTAGES
1. The setter releases from the backcourt, which means they must cover more ground to get to the target area.
2. Since setters try to release quickly, there is a potential for overlap if the setter releases and overlaps another player before the contact on the serve.

79

THE 5-1 OFFENSE

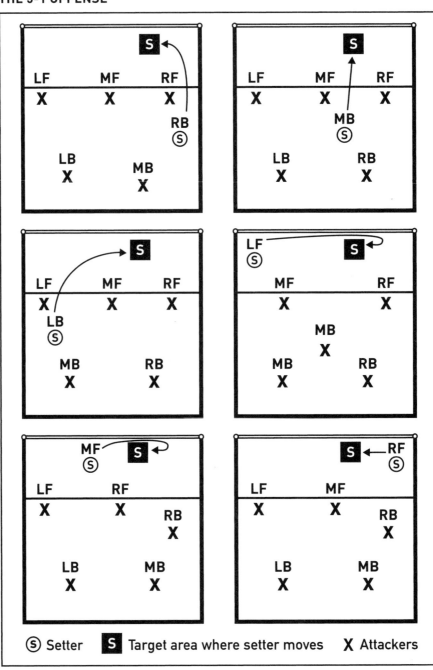

THE 5-1 OFFENSE
(COMBINATION OF THE FRONT AND BACK-ROW SYSTEMS)

In a 5-1 offense, there are five attackers and one setter. When the setter is in the back row, a 6-2 system is used. When the setter is in the front row, a 4-2 system is used. Since one person is responsible for all the setting, that person obviously has to be very efficient at setting—and very quick.

ADVANTAGES
1. Consistency of sets is a big advantage to this system. With one setter being responsible to set all the balls, the hitters don't have to adapt as much to where the balls are being set.
2. Setters can become attackers when they are at the net by hitting the pass over the net instead of setting. This can be used as a surprise attack that keeps the defense on their toes.

DISADVANTAGES
1. When the setter is in the front row, there are only two attackers unless the setter attacks the pass.
2. If the setter is not a good blocker, the defense can be compromised when the setter is in the front row.

THE 6-6 AND 6-3 OFFENSIVE SYSTEMS

In a 6-6 system, there are six hitters and six setters. When players rotate to a particular position (usually right back or right front), they become the setter for that one rotation. In a 6-3 system, three players set in two rotations, either when they are right back and middle back or right front and right back. These innovative systems work well in youth volleyball since they help to develop multiple skills in young players.

OFFENSIVE CONCEPTS

When working offense with young athletes, it is important to emphasize three contacts on your side (pass, set, and spike). Most coaches will teach this to their athletes, but when it comes to game time, the kids get rewarded by passing the ball over the net on the first contact or shooting the ball over on the second contact continuously if it results in a point or a sideout. Most of this reinforcement comes from the crowd, which is made up of energetic parents. This is one of the hardest concepts to teach young kids when they first start to play the game, because it is harder for young kids to control three contacts than it is to play the ball over the net on the first or second contact. It takes a patient and conscientious coach to get the team to the point where they want to do the skills right and play the game properly more than they want to win. Besides educating the kids on this concept of three hits on one side, the parents must also be educated. They need to know it's more important that the kids learn how to play the game correctly than it is to win. After all, how many teams are successful playing the ball over on the first or second contact at the high school and college level? Zero. Therefore, the coach, athletes, and parents must work through this transitional stage and support the kids' efforts to play the game correctly. Otherwise, they will jeopardize their future in the sport.

THE FULL-COURT ATTACK

We introduced this concept to our kids when they were seven years old. Most offenses use only the front-row players as attackers. We have observed that young kids lose their concentration when not actively involved in the game. At times with very young players, the only alert kids are the ones in the front row because they are ready to hit. The back-row players are either asleep or have taken a concentration break. Therefore, we introduced a full-court attack, which uses all players on the court as potential attackers, whether they are in the front or back row. When a back-row player attacks the ball, she may not jump in front of the attack line, but that does not mean she cannot hit. What is interesting about young kids is that it is actually

FULL-COURT ATTACK

In a full-court attack, all players may attack the ball, including the back-row players, as long as they do not jump in front of the attack line on the take-off. Notice in this picture that the center back player is attacking the ball. The player may land in front of the attack line after the ball is hit.

82

easier for them to hit a deep set than it is to hit a set closer to the net. So including a back row attack is a natural for young teams. It helps to keep their concentration, and it is easier for them to hit the ball in the court. It also gives the setter more options and can help the offense be strong on a pass that does not make it to the target area. The backcourt set should be directed to the attack line in the seam between the front-row attackers.

OFFENSIVE STRATEGY

Once you have your receive pattern, your offensive system, and your team's ability to make three contacts on its side, it is time to think about where you will attack the opposing team's defense. Besides being able to hit the ball in the court consistently, your players should eventually be able to attack the opposing team's holes. This requires that the athletes can hit both straight ahead and to various angles that would send the ball either crosscourt or down the line into the defender's court. The athletes should also be able to tip the ball into the holes left by the block and be able to hit off the blockers' hands. These techniques can be worked on by setting up targets on the court during practice and requiring the athletes to hit at the targets.

HITTER COVERAGE

Besides attacking various positions on the opponent's court, another area a coach needs to be aware of is the opposing block (if there is one). If the opposing team has a big block, your team needs to be able to cover the hitters in case the ball is blocked back to your side of the court. Proper hitter coverage is shown in the illustration on page 84. The players are positioned during the spike in the area to which the ball will most likely be blocked. If your players retrieve the blocked ball, they can continue the rally and, at the same time, make the blockers on the other side of the court seem ineffective.

The bottom line with team offense is to choose the best patterns and systems that will work for you and your team. In a nutshell, one word says it all—consistency.

HITTER COVERAGE

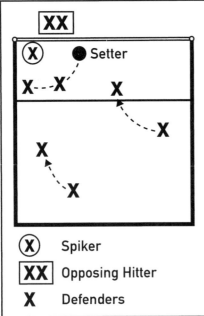

The three closest players to the spiker form a short cup behind the spiker. The other two players fill in the deep seams. All players assume a low position and watch the ball as it contacts the opposing block. If the hitter is blocked, they will try to retrieve the ball to the setter to initiate another attack.

Ⓧ	Spiker
XX	Opposing Hitter
X	Defenders

BASIC DEFENSE

07

Defense in volleyball is what separates good teams from great teams. You could have the best hitters and setters around, but if they can't play defense, your team will struggle to win games. Defense involves digging, blocking (when appropriate), and transition, where the setter sets the dig to an attacker. You will not score very many points against a good team unless your team can play defense. Most youth coaches spend the majority of their practice time on offense because that's what the kids like the most. Everyone likes to hit, and if it were up to the kids, that's all they would do at practice. However, they will never get to hit in a game unless they can pass and dig, and digging is a lot tougher than passing because it is more difficult to dig a spike than it is to pass a serve. When your team is serving, players must be ready to play defense if the other team receives the serve and sends it back over with an attack. Also, when the other team serves, once your team's offense returns the ball to the opponent, your team must play defense for the remainder of the rally. Therefore, most of the time, your team is going to be playing defense.

It is important that athletes understand where to go on defense and how to play their positions. They must also have good defensive techniques, such as digging, sprawl-

DEFENSE

Moving to the ball and digging are the key elements to any defensive system.

ing and rolling, and if appropriate, blocking techniques. These techniques are explained in detail in chapter four.

HOW TO SET UP A DEFENSE

When working with beginning players, you need to keep the defense as simple as possible. As players progress more in their movement and skills, the defense can become more intricate and challenging based on your team's strengths and weaknesses. We recommend the following basic defenses to take your team from the most beginning level to the high school level.

FIVE-PERSON BACK DEFENSE (NO-BLOCK DEFENSE)

This defense resembles a five-person receive pattern with the setter at the net. There are no blockers in this defense. The players assume the same positions as they would in a five-person receive pattern, and the setter at the net gives the diggers a target. The only difference between the service receive pattern and the defense pattern is that the players need to be physically lower to the ground to play the ball and must read the opposing hitter within their respective positions.

ADVANTAGES
1. This is the easiest defense to teach young kids and gives them the greatest chance of success.
2. This is also the safest defense for young kids since there is no blocking. This cuts down on the risk of injury.

DISADVANTAGES
1. At some point, your athletes will ideally outgrow this defense. This usually happens by age fourteen.
2. When you start playing against teams that can attack the ball from above the net with a lot of force, it will become very difficult to dig these balls, and you will eventually need to incorporate a block (or buy some crash helmets).

TIPS FOR TEACHING THIS DEFENSE
1. Make sure your players watch the opposing hitter and react to the ball.
2. Demand that they start from a low base position and step at the ball.

FIVE-PERSON BACK DEFENSE

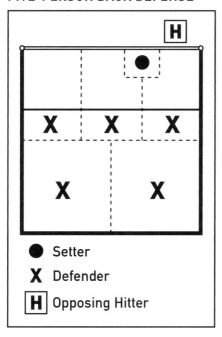

In the five-person back defense, five players cover the court on defense while the setter is in position at the net to set the dig. The general areas the diggers are responsible for are indicated. If a ball is between two players, the one who is moving toward the setter has priority to dig the ball.

● Setter

X Defender

H Opposing Hitter

DEFENSE SPECIALIZATION

As players start to develop, you can have them specialize at a particular defensive position. The players you have identified as setters will usually play right back, or behind the block, when they are in the back row and up at the net at the target area or in the right-front position if your team is blocking when they are in the front row. The players you think will eventually become middle blockers will switch to the middle positions on defense, either the middle front or middle back depending on whether they are in the front or back row at the time. The outside hitters will switch to left front when they are in the front row and most likely left back when they are in the back row. This puts your players in the same defensive positions each time, which will make them more familiar with its demands and put them in their most advantageous position to attack the ball if the team is successful in digging the opposing team's attack. Liberos and defensive specialists should be able to play all three back-row positions. You can introduce defense specialization even before the team is ready to use a blocking defense so they are used to the switches before you have to think about adding a block. Remember, the team must rotate each position before the serve, but they can stay in their defensive

87

positions until the rally is over. Once the rally is over, the players must assume their correct rotational order until the serve is contacted again. When working with children, this will be confusing at first. They will look at you with horror and ask, "Where do I go?" This is another reason why defense needs a lot of work at practice.

WHEN TO INCORPORATE BLOCKING INTO YOUR DEFENSE

It seems ridiculous to have kids trying to block who cannot get their hands above the net, but a lot of coaches have their teams do this because they think it is how the game needs to be played. My philosophy is that you don't have kids block until they can be successful at it. I can't tell you how easy it is to beat a team that tries to block before they are ready. Talk about holes in the defense! However, around the ages of thirteen and fourteen, some kids are ready to block. It is unusual to have a team this age that can all get above the net to block, but you can set up a defense that will allow some kids to block and others to stay down on defense. This defense is called a 1-2, 1-2.

THE 1-1, 2-2 DEFENSE

This defense is considered a transitional defense because it is a bridge between a no-block defense and a regular two-person blocking defense. It is useful because it allows coaches to begin teaching blocking without sacrificing a lot of court for the other team to attack.

In this defense, there is one blocker at the net who attempts to block the opposing team's attackers. This person starts close to the net and moves along the net to whatever position the opposing attacker is hitting from. The other two frontcourt players drop to the attack line to dig, just like they would in the five-person back defense. The setter plays in the middle position, at the attack line behind the blocker, and is in position to dig the tips. If another player digs the ball, the setter releases to the target area to set the attack. If the setter digs the ball, an alternate setter must be identified by the coach (usually the right-front player). The other two back-row players split the court and dig the deep ball.

ADVANTAGES
1. This defense will help you use taller kids who might take away some of the opposing team's hitting angles.
2. It will sometimes distract the opposing hitters if they are not used to hitting against a block.
3. It is a balanced defense that does not have many holes for the opposing team to attack.

1-1, 2-2 DEFENSE

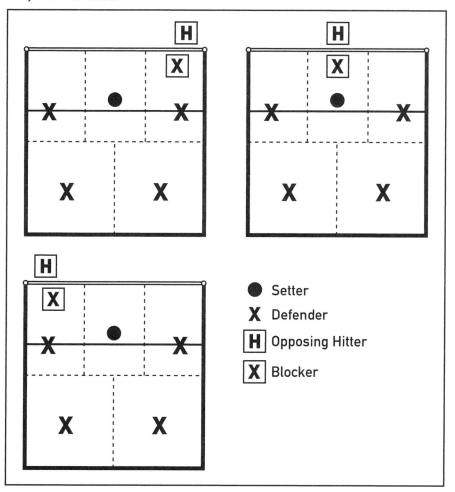

The 1-1, 2-2 defense uses one blocker at the net. The two other front-row players drop off to the attack line. The back-row setter plays the center position at the attack line while the other two back-row players split the backcourt. The area each player defends is indicated.

DISADVANTAGES

1. When using only one blocker at the net, the player needs to determine which balls to try to block and which to not block. The deeper sets off the net would not necessitate a block and would call for the blocker to stay down (not block) or retreat off the net to play defense.

2. If the blocker backs off the net, the setter must immediately release to the target area. As a coach, this takes a lot of time to teach and can be very frustrating when the athletes are first learning it.

TIPS FOR TEACHING THIS DEFENSE
1. Practice situations that require a block and those that do not.
2. Hit balls at the players from across the net, and also toss balls similar to free balls that will require the blocker to back off the net to play defense.

BLOCKING DEFENSES

When your players are tall enough to block, or can get their hands above the net, it is time to teach a blocking defense that uses more than one blocker at the net. There are several to choose from, such as the man up, perimeter, and rover. We recommend the rotational defense, since it has the least amount of holes in it for the other team to attack.

THE ROTATIONAL DEFENSE

This defense is designed to place two blockers at the position of the opponent's attack and have the remaining four players rotate to predetermined positions on the court. The players move from a basic starting position to a defensive position based on the direction of the opposing set and the position of the hitter.

In this defense, the middle blocker moves next to the outside blocker who positions the block on the opposing hitter's shoulder. They will form a double block in front of the opposing attacker. The back-row player directly behind the outside blocker moves up to the attack line to defend the tip. The middle back rotates to the sideline while the other back-row defender rotates to the middle of the court. The off-blocker (the third front-row player who is not part of the block) pulls back to the attack line to prepare to dig the hard balls hit to the angle.

ADVANTAGES
1. This defense keeps the players moving and concentrating on the hitter. There is no standing still on this defense.
2. It is difficult to find holes in this defense if it is properly executed. The power hits are covered and so is the tip.

DISADVANTAGES
1. If the blockers cannot put up an effective block, several holes will open up.
2. This defense will not work with slow or inattentive defenders.

ROTATIONAL-BLOCKING DEFENSE

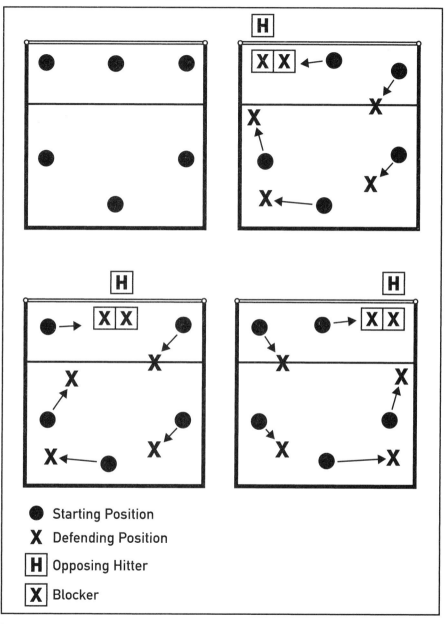

● Starting Position

X Defending Position

H Opposing Hitter

X Blocker

The rotational-blocking defense uses two blockers at the net, while the other players rotate into their defensive positions based on the opposition's attack. The arrows show the direction the players will rotate depending upon the direction of the attack.

TIPS FOR TEACHING THIS DEFENSE

1. The defenders must be challenged when teaching this defense. This is no time to hit easy balls at the defense.
2. Use a chair and hit the balls from above the net into areas you know are weak.

FINAL THOUGHTS

Whatever defense is used, the team must be comfortable and familiar with it. This takes time, especially with younger athletes. Nothing is more frustrating than to have players look at each other or look at you and continue to ask, "Whose ball was that?" They need to know this before the games, and it needs to be worked on at practice.

TRAINING YOUR TEAM

08

Basically, a coach's job takes place at practice. Once a team is involved in a game, the only things a coach can do are turn in the lineup, call a limited amount of time-outs, make substitutions, and talk to the kids before and after the games. The kids are either in control or totally out of control. The old saying "practice makes perfect" may be somewhat exaggerated, but you can expect teams to perform better in the matches if they have worked hard at practice.

Our philosophy is that practice is work, and the game is the time for the kids to have fun and see how well they can perform. Some coaches goof around at practice, then get upset when game time comes and the kids don't perform. If the kids don't perform at practice, what makes you think they will do well when they play against

TRAINING

Being a coach means you sometimes must get actively involved at the practices. Spiking a ball at the defense can be aided by the use of a chair or stool.

another team? It's like being in a concert or a play. Your kids should practice so they will have the confidence to do well when it's "showtime."

Getting your athletes "game ready" is a big responsibility. They must be confident in their abilities and each other. Several drills that can be used at practice, both for competitive and recreational situations, are included in this chapter. When putting a practice session together, the coach can be creative and use varied drills specific to the team's needs but should keep in mind four basic components of training the volleyball athlete: specific conditioning, fundamentals, teamwork, and competition training. They are all important.

SPECIFIC CONDITIONING

Conditioning gets the body ready for the physical demands of the sport. The body needs to be warmed up and, ideally, specific muscles should be stretched before and after the workout. The actual conditioning phase should not be overemphasized. I have seen many coaches go nuts in this area and try to use conditioning to weed out the weak players or establish discipline. Sometimes, they will make their teams run for hours or do all sorts of exercises that have little or nothing to do with the physical demands of the sport. As a result, the majority of the practice time is wasted.

There is a training principle with which all physical educators and fitness specialists are very familiar. It is called *specificity*. In a nutshell, this means the training for the sport should match the physical demands of the activity. Only then can the training be transferred to the sport. If you are engaged in a sport requiring quickness and power, the conditioning training should match those demands. In a sport like volleyball, there is jumping, squatting, and short sprinting. It is played on a small surface and is an anaerobic sport (stop and go). In a sport such as this, the conditioning phase should emphasize jump training, leg strength, upper-body strength, sprint training, and anaerobic interval work. However, many youth coaches make their teams run for long distances. Even if this is combined with the correct conditioning, it is training the muscles the opposite way. Volleyball, and sports like it, trains the fast-twitch muscle fibers in the body. Running distances will break these down and actually decrease an athlete's jump and speed. If you are going to incorporate a lot of conditioning, make sure it is going to help the athletes perform better at their sport, not work against them. Since you are working with a ball sport, add conditioning drills that include the ball. Not only are these efficient, they're also fun. There are drills included in this chapter that show you how to kill these two birds with one stone.

FUNDAMENTALS

Most kids and coaches don't like to spend time on fundamentals such as footwork, serving, or passing because they think they are boring. Many youth coaches just let the team play games against each other at practice, because that's what everyone likes the most. However, fundamentals are the basic skills of the sport, and they need to be reviewed frequently so kids can play the sport better and have more fun. I have seen many kids thrust into competition before they knew how to actually perform any of the skills correctly; it was incredibly frustrating to watch from the stands, and I'm sure even more frustrating for the players on the court.

All kids want to play, but to be successful they must first learn how to do the skills correctly. A coach needs to break down the basics of the sport and make sure each kid has at least some proficiency in each skill before there are any performance expectations on the part of the coach, kid, or parent. It takes a while for a person to learn a new skill because the brain has to be trained and conditioned before the movement will be smooth. Coaches working with small children have a major responsibility to teach the fundamentals correctly so the kids will not have to break bad habits for the rest of their volleyball careers. Fundamentals always need to be reviewed. Even college and professional players spend a lot of time reviewing fundamentals, so youth coaches must incorporate this into their training.

Drills that emphasize fundamentals can be fun with a little innovation on the part of the coach. Drills for each of the fundamentals with variations are included in this chapter.

TEAMWORK

The larger the team, the more practice time needs to be spent on teamwork. It takes a lot of time to figure out what positions each kid will play and how to get the team to work together. Try to get kids in the positions where they will have the most success. Make sure you try them in several positions, and take into consideration where they feel the most comfortable. With very young kids, it is recommended they learn how to play all the positions. As the team starts to specialize in positions, make sure you have objective reasons why certain kids should play certain positions. Make all the positions seem equally important. The setter, libero, and defensive specialist should always be made to feel they contribute as much to the team as the middle and outside hitters.

Practice drills can be set up either with the whole team or using the part-whole method. Putting a whole team out on the court before the kids know where to go can be confusing. Work them in small groups first then work up to the full team. This part-whole method also works for older teams when you need to work on a particular part of the offense or defense. Break it down to two-on-two, three-on-three, etc. Kids will also get to know their teammates better and become more confident in their skills if they work in smaller groups first. Team drills on defense, offense, and transition included in this chapter can either be done with a full team or using the part-whole method by reducing the number of players in the drill and working a certain area of the court.

COMPETITION TRAINING

We hear coaches say this all the time: "My team practices so well, but when we get to the games, they just fall apart." This is not unusual, especially if the competition element is relatively new to the kids. Prepare your team for competition by incorporating competition into your practice. This type of training can be used at the recreational level, but it is more important at the competitive level. Bring competition into practices by using "against" drills, where your players are pitted against each other and you keep score and declare a winner at the end of the drill. These situations are usually fun for the kids as long as you don't do them too often. Another variation of competition training is reality work, where the group or person performs a certain preset number of skills correctly in a row (like serving ten balls in a row in the court, as a group or individually).

Bringing in another team to play yours is a good idea, especially before the first tournament or game. A lot can be learned at a scrimmage and can be practiced before the team has to do it for real in a game or a tournament. You can also prepare your athletes at practice by telling them what to expect at the competition so there is no uncertainty. This is where scouting other teams can be of value. For example, if a team sends the ball over the net on the first or second contact consistently, and your team knows this ahead of time, they will be ready for it.

Where you are in your season will determine how much time will be spent on these four areas. At the beginning of the season, most of the time should be spent on fundamentals and some specific conditioning. As the competitions get closer, more time needs to be spent on teamwork and competition readiness. After each game, the coach should work on the team's weaknesses to get them prepared for the next match.

SAMPLE PRACTICE

Here is an example of how to put together a two-hour practice session:

    10 minutes: Warm-up (slow jogging, jumping, footwork, stretching)

    10 minutes: Serving

    10 minutes: Passing

    10 minutes: Setting

    10 minutes: Spiking

    10 minutes: Individual defense (digging, sprawl, roll, block rebound, etc.)

    15 minutes: Team offense (smaller groups, three to four players)

    25 minutes: Team defense (smaller groups, three to four players)

    20 minutes: Transition, against drills, or scrimmage

DRILLS

The following drills can be incorporated at practice. They are simple to run and cover every aspect of the game. There are also variations for the drills depending on the age and skill level of the athletes.

SERVING DRILLS

When working with the younger athletes or the beginners, move them closer to the net. Once they have success serving the ball over the net and have demonstrated good technique, move them slowly back to the end line. Remember, serving is mostly concentration. Do not allow your kids to goof around when serving. Watch their form and give them feedback.

The serve-and-shag drill allows the coach to watch the server's form and incorporates conditioning as well, since he must run to shag (retrieve) the ball when he goes to the opposite line. This drill can also be a reality drill if you demand efficiency before the team goes on to the next drill.

The serving-pairs competition drill adds a competitive element to serving and adds target serving since the goal of this drill is to have the kids serve to an assigned area of the court. Use chairs as targets or, for a real incentive, you be the target.

PASSING DRILLS

The two-ball passing drill requires the players to move into position to pass the ball. For beginning players, make the tosses easy and allow plenty of time for them to get to the ball. For more advanced players, serve tougher and make them move farther to

SERVE-AND-SHAG DRILL

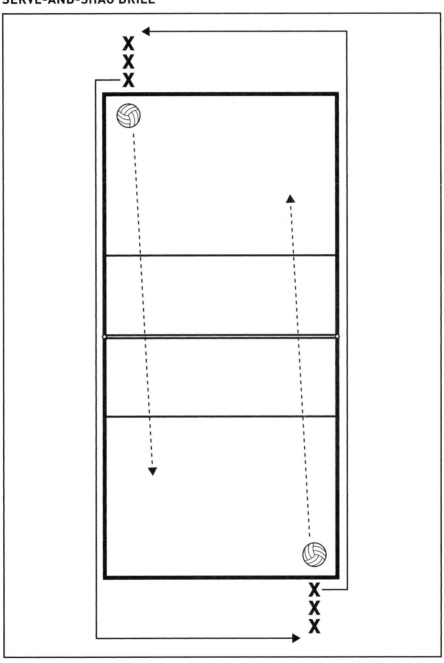

SERVING-PAIRS COMPETITION DRILL

TWO-BALL PASSING DRILL

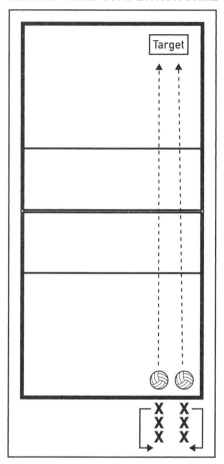

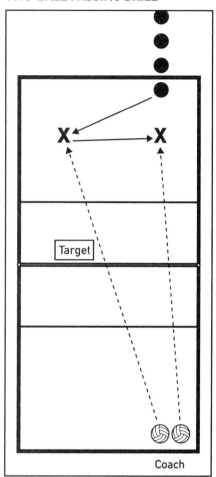

In the serving-pairs competition two teams play to 10 points. Each team member earns a point for successfully serving a target, which can be placed anywhere on the other side of the court. The first team to ten wins. Serving accuracy, competition and teamwork are stressed in this drill.

In the two-ball passing drill the coach serves or tosses a ball crosscourt. The first player in line moves to the ball and passes to the target. The coach then serves or tosses to the line. The same player moves to the ball, passes to the target and then returns to the line. Repeat. This drill emphasizes movement and passing accuracy.

◄ The server serves the ball, runs to the other side of the court, retrieves it and gets into the opposite line to prepare to serve again. As a variation, since the serving rule change, you can allow players to serve anywhere along the endline so they don't have to wait in line. Repeat for ten minutes, allowing the player to try various serves. This drill teaches correct serving technique and reinforces concentration when players are winded, since they are running to get into position to serve.

pass the ball. This drill can be varied by having the kids toss the balls when you have more than one passing group. If you choose this option, make sure you supervise this drill so the kids will keep their concentration.

The Three-Person Passing Drill

In this drill, the emphasis is on communication between players and efficiency. The coach puts three players on the opposite side of the court. Each player is responsible for one-third of the court: one on the right, one in the middle, and one on the left. The coach randomly serves to different parts of the court. Passers communicate, move to, and pass the balls to the target. They complete ten passes and then change players. This drill can be done with easy tosses or serves for the beginning players, or for the more advanced players, the coach can serve tough and demand a certain number of passes before the group changes. A competitive variation of this drill is to have the athletes serve instead of the coach and the servers and the passers compete as teams. The first team to either get ten aces or ten successful passes wins.

SETTING DRILLS

The four-person setting drill is an excellent way to get all of your players proficient at setting. They must use their hands in this drill. If they cannot set the ball, they must catch it because there will be a tendency to forearm pass the balls they feel they cannot set. This drill teaches them to move to the ball. The coach must observe and give positive feedback about how the players are handling the ball.

SPIKING DRILLS

In the progression spiking drill, spiking is taught and drilled in a three-part progression. Begin by lining up the players at left front, middle front, or right front. Toss the ball to the first player in line who, from a standing position, takes a step with the foot opposite the spiking hand and employs the arm-swing technique and hits the ball over the net into the opponent's court. The spiker shags the ball and returns to the line.

Once the players have been successful hitting the ball over the net, move on to part two. Toss the ball to the spiker, who uses a two-step approach technique and jumps and hits the ball into the opponent's court. In part three, toss the ball to the spiker, who uses a three-step approach and arm-swing technique to hit the ball into the opponent's court. To review the two-step and three-step approach and the arm swing, refer to chapter four. The coach needs to make sure the kids hit the bottom third of the ball, snap over the top, and use the correct footwork. Once this progression is intact, the drill can be

FOUR-PERSON SETTING DRILL

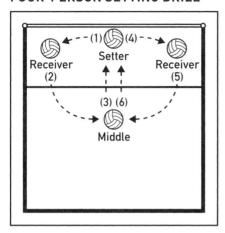

The four-person front- and back-setting drill is a continuous moving drill. The setter sets forward (straight ahead) (1), receiver sets to the middle (2), middle sets to the setter (3), the setter sets backward (4), the receiver sets to the middle (5), and the middle sets to the setter (6). Repeat for twelve sets by the setter and then switch setters. To add difficulty for more advanced players, have the setter slide back to the attack line after each set so they are moving to the ball.

varied by having smaller groups hit at a time (usually three) or emphasize target hitting or tipping. The drill can also be varied by tossing the ball to a setter who sets the balls to the hitters, or having the hitters pass the ball to the setter before they hit.

THE STAND-AND-BLOCK DRILL

This drill emphasizes blocking form. Stand on a chair or platform and spike ten consecutive balls to a blocker who is positioned on the other side of the net. Repeat the drill with another blocker. For safety, assign a "foot watcher" who makes sure no balls are near the blocker's feet when he is jumping. For beginners, hit all ten balls straight ahead. For intermediate players, tell your player which angle will be hit before you hit the ball. For advanced players, randomly hit balls at all possible angles. For shorter players, you can lower the net or string some rope at a lower height so they work at correct technique without worrying about getting above the net. Correct blocking technique needs to be emphasized. You need to be warned that a lot of kids will try to block the ball into your head (which is considered a good block).

THE BLOCK-MOVE-BLOCK DRILL

This drill emphasizes blocking and correct footwork. Stand on a chair or platform about two feet from the sideline, right at the net. Position a player across the net from you. Spike the ball to the player, who should attempt to block it, then sidestep to the near sideline and slide-step back to position. As the player returns to position, spike the ball again for her to block before she crossover steps toward the far sideline and crossover steps back. Spike the ball to the player as she returns. Repeat this process ten times before changing players.

DEFENSIVE DRILLS

The next four drills work individual defensive skills. Like the spiking progression, the first drill emphasizes correct technique.

The Undercut Drill

In the undercut drill, line four players up in the center of the court. You are at the net on the same side of the court. Using two hands, push a fast ball at knee height of the first player in line. The player steps at the ball, drops his hips below the ball, undercuts the ball and scoops it to the target. Repeat the drill with the next player in line. Correct technique for the undercut can be found in chapter four. This drill can be modified into a rebound drill, sprawl drill, or roll drill depending on what defensive technique the coach wishes to teach. The only difference is where the ball is tossed.

The Defensive Scoop Drill

In this drill, the coach challenges the athlete with the undercut and scoop by adding movement.

The Basic-Read Drill

The basic-read drill emphasizes movement to the ball and reading the hitter. Any of the defensive techniques can be used to dig the ball. To make this drill more challenging, hit the ball harder or to the front or side of the players so they will have to use a sprawl

DEFENSIVE SCOOP DRILL

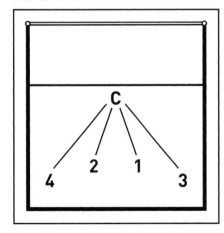

Push ball 1 at digger's right knee. Digger steps to ball, drops hips under ball, and scoops ball to coach. Repeat with ball 2 at digger's left knee. Then toss ball 3 wide to right of digger. Digger steps laterally to right and scoops ball to coach. Repeat with ball 4 wide to left of digger.

BASIC-READ DRILL

FIRST-TURN DRILL

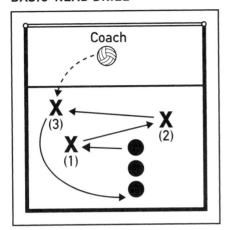

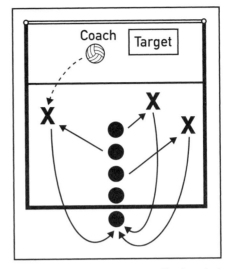

Stand at the net and line up four players at the center of the court. As you turn to your right, the first player moves and positions her nose to your hitting shoulder. As you turn to the left, the player moves to the digging position, again with her nose to your shoulder. Turn one more time, either to the right or the left, and this time, spike the ball. The player moves to position and digs the ball back to you. Repeat this process with the next players.

In the first-turn drill, players are lined up similar to the basic-read drill. The coach turns to the right and spikes the ball. The first digger moves to position and digs the ball to the target, then returns to line. The coach turns to the left and spikes the ball. The second digger moves to position and digs the ball to the target and returns to line. The coach and subsequent diggers repeat the process. An odd number of players in line is desirable so players can dig from both right and left sides of the court.

or a roll. Players who are not in the drill will have to help with the shagging and the feeding (retrieving balls and handing them to the coach).

The First-Turn Drill

The first-turn drill is by far the fastest and the most fun for the kids. Make sure you have a person who will hand you the balls quickly and that you have a lot of shaggers to retrieve balls so you can keep the drill going. Kids love this drill.

WORKING TEAM OFFENSE

The team-offense drill works the team against a server on the other side of the court. The coach serves the ball, and the team passes, sets, and hits the ball over the net.

Remember to emphasize three contacts. For beginning players, keep the serves easy so they can have success. As the players get more competent, you can serve tougher and to the weak areas on the court. Also, you can have your athletes serve, especially if they serve tougher than you do. This drill can be varied by using smaller groups, such as four people instead of six, to work on particular areas of the court.

WORKING TEAM DEFENSE

The team-defense drill works the team against an attack. Usually, the coach is on a chair and hits the ball at various places on the court. The team digs the ball and tries to play it out (set the dig and hit it over). For beginners, the coach should hit the ball easy so the kids can be successful. This drill can be used to work down ball and free-ball situations with a team that must make decisions about whether to block a particular attack.

THE TRANSITION DRILL

This drill pits two teams or two groups against each other. Position yourself behind the sideline (out of bounds) at the net. Toss the ball to either team. They should pass, set, and hit to the opponent's court. The defense digs and transitions the ball back, and play continues until the rally ends. Each time the ball hits the floor or goes out you immediately toss the ball to the winning team until one team earns 15 or 25 points. You can vary this drill by using only four players on each side of the court. This approach allows you to focus on the hitting and defending the line or crosscourt. There is usually no time to make corrections in this drill, since it works best if it is nonstop. Make sure you mix up your groups so all kids can have success. This drill is usually a hit with the kids if they all have a chance to win.

The bottom line on training your team is to use your practice time well. The kids should enjoy the workout, but they must also concentrate. You should devote extra time working on whatever weaknesses your team has. You want your team to be confident when it comes to game time and be able to enjoy the game to its fullest.

NUTRITIONAL CONCERNS

Even if you have excellent training techniques, your team might not perform to their potential if they do not eat properly. Most kids have poor nutritional habits. As a coach, you are not responsible for what they eat, but you can make them more aware of how important it is to eat right, especially when it comes to being an athlete.

TEAM-OFFENSE DRILL

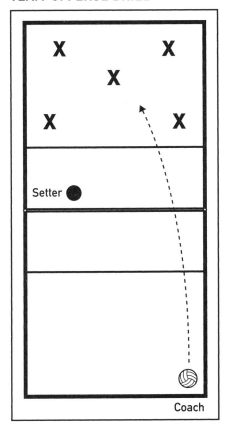

TEAM-DEFENSE DRILL

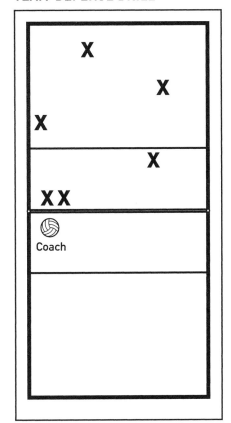

To practice team offense, serve ten balls to a receiving team of five passers and a setter. Players should execute a pass, set, and attack each time. Players rotate every ten plays. To make this more challenging, add blockers to your side of the net. Start serving easy, and then serve tougher as the team is successful. You can also experiment with other receive patterns such as the four-, three-, or two-person receive.

To practice team defense, spike ten balls to the defending team who digs and transitions the ball each time. After ten reps, repeat the drill from the middle and right side. As a variation, have the players hit to the defense while you set the hitters, or you can toss to a setter while three hitters attack the defense. You can add a competitive element to this drill by keeping score.

This might seem irrelevant to you, but kids' performances on the court might very well be influenced by what they have eaten or not eaten previously. Kids can run out of energy, become ill, or be so hyperactive that they lose the ability to concentrate. You want them to have the best chance to succeed. Remember, you can train them all you want, but if they don't have the proper fuel their chances of performing well are significantly reduced.

It's possible the kids on your team have all sorts of nutritional deficiencies. Most food is made to look good, taste good, and be easy to prepare, with little regard to nutritional value. As a result, most foods are laden with fat and sugar and devoid of nutrients because of overprocessing. Children are trusting and will eat what is put in front of them most of the time, so it's up to the adults to teach kids good nutritional habits. Since most of our habits start when we are kids, now is the time to make a good impression.

Why is this of concern to you? For one thing, you can make an impression on kids about how important it is to eat right. Teach them to respect their bodies and watch what they put into them. Let them know the foods they should stay away from prior to a competition and what sort of foods they should eat. They will usually listen to you if you think it is important. Who knows? It might even rub off on some of the parents.

FOODS TO STAY AWAY FROM BEFORE THE GAME

1. Sugary foods and drinks will elevate blood glucose, which will set off an insulin reaction in the body. In about thirty minutes, the blood sugar level will drop, causing fatigue. Obviously, you don't want kids to be tired when they need to have the most energy.
2. Carbonated drinks can cause gastrointestinal distress. Kids' stomachs will hurt because of gas. Also, if there is caffeine in the drink, it might cause dehydration, which can be serious if the weather is hot.
3. High-protein and fatty foods will stay in the stomach for long periods of time and cause discomfort and lethargy if they are eaten too close to game time. Protein foods would be more appropriate after the games to help them recover.

WHAT SHOULD THEY EAT?

An hour or two before the game, the team should have foods high in complex carbohydrates. These would include breads, cereals, pasta, vegetables, and fruit. They should never compete if they haven't had anything to eat. A little bit of protein can be added, which would include meats like turkey or chicken (red meat is also protein but might be too heavy for some kids).

On the day of the game, we find that a team cooler is a great way to make sure good foods are available for the athletes. You can assign a parent who will delegate different parents to bring certain foods. Our typical sign-up sheet looks like this:

1. Fruit juice
2. Fruits
3. Bagels and cream cheese
4. Bread and lunch meats
5. Crackers and cheese
6. Cookies and brownies (you have to live a little)
7. Yogurt
8. Sports drinks/thirst quenchers or similar mineral replacements
9. Water
10. Ice
11. Muffins
12. Vegetables and dip

You can be a good example to your team if you eat well. Remember, "Do what I say, not what I do" never works with kids.

FLUID REPLACEMENT

Water makes up about 60 percent of our body weight. Fluid replacement is critical to the health of your athletes. Satisfying thirst will only satisfy one-third of their fluid requirements. An athlete needs at least six to ten glasses of water a day. Water should never be restricted from an athlete. It should always be provided and the athlete should be allowed to drink whenever he needs it. Coaches who do not allow their athletes to drink water during practice or competitions are endangering their athletes' health.

Sports Drinks

There are several sports drinks on the market that are highly promoted for athletes. Most of them contain carbohydrates, vitamins, and minerals, and some contain amino acids, which are the building blocks of proteins. These drinks might be appropriate for all-day tournaments and might help the athletes toward the end of the day replace the minerals they might have lost through sweating. However, they should not replace water. If you decide to have your team use these supplemental drinks, make sure they are also drinking water. Also, some of the more concentrated drinks would be better off diluted for younger kids (one part drink, one part water).

In summary, you really do not have much control in the area of nutrition for your kids. All you can do is make recommendations and be a good example. However, you should never tell a kid that she should go on a diet or that she needs to lose weight.

This could plant a seed for a major eating disorder. Instead try to promote healthy eating habits and a respect for her body.

Training your team is the most important part of your job. Time is valuable. Remember to give lots of feedback and give positive reinforcement when your athletes do things correctly. Don't become a nag and focus on what they're doing wrong. Reward good technique and keep instructing your athletes on proper footwork and skill. Focus more on ball-handling skills and teamwork than conditioning. With the rally scoring system, the best-conditioned team will always be defeated by the team with the best skills.

PRIVATE COACHING AND TRAINING

A growing trend in today's game, in addition to school and club practices and competitions, is for coaches to require and parents to hire personal trainers and private coaching to give their athletes an edge. There are pros and cons to these practices.

PROS

Personal Training: improved strength, agility, quickness, speed, and jump as well as providing for injury prevention

Private Coaching: skill improvement

CONS

Personal Training: possibility of burnout and overtraining as well as injury if not done properly

Private Coaching: burnout; an inconsistency in coaching by learning skills improperly or differently than the style of the school/club coach

It is important to do your homework in researching and getting recommendations regarding the expertise and style of personal trainers and private coaches. It is also very important that the athlete wants this extra help and is excited and enthused about the opportunity to work with the additional help.

PERFORMANCE TRAINING: A PROFESSIONAL'S PERSPECTIVE

By Ken Vick
Sports Performance Director, Velocity Sports Performance

WHY PERFORMANCE TRAINING?

While developing volleyball skills will do the most to help an athlete improve and enjoy the game, sports performance training will keep him healthier, injury free, and increase his capacity to practice and play the game.

It's about building overall athleticism and physical capacity. That way, when an athlete walks out onto the court, whether it's to practice or compete, she can focus on volleyball instead of worrying about being limited by physical restrictions. Improving one's game is the biggest motivation for undertaking a performance training program. In volleyball, jumping higher and getting quicker are usually involved. All of these athletic qualities can be improved. While an athlete may not have the genetics to jump like a national team player, every athlete at any age can train and improve his jump and quickness.

Another big motivator is injury prevention. Whether it's so injuries never happen or to prevent them from happening again, the right performance training can significantly reduce the risk of injury. By improving athleticism, increasing strength and power qualities, and building stability and mobility, an athlete is more prepared to play.

FINDING A SPORTS PERFORMANCE PROGRAM

Once an athlete has decided to start a sports performance program, she needs to figure out how to get started. Here are some points to keep in mind.

PERFORMANCE COACH OR DO-IT-YOURSELF

An athlete goes into performance training in either one of two ways: by finding a coach or doing it alone. There are advantages and disadvantages to each. The important questions need to be answered honestly so good results occur.

A good sports performance coach gives an athlete the advantage of expertise in learning exercises and selecting the best ones. Since every person has unique qualities, goals, injury history, and personality, programs need to be fit to each individual. The drawback is that it comes with cost. While it varies from region to region, forty to seventy-five dollars is a common per-session rate. Many performance coaches and training centers offer small-group training with two to six athletes that can be motivating and more affordable.

Doing it alone without a performance coach has the advantage of a lower cost, making it work when and the way one wants and the satisfaction of doing it. The drawback is that if an athlete doesn't have specific knowledge, it is nearly impossible to do it well. Following a program designed by others, from a DVD, book, or seminar is a better approach. The challenge is making sure good technique is used and that things are done properly.

VOLLEYBALL SPECIFIC

A volleyball athlete needs a volleyball performance coach, right? Wrong. A volleyball athlete needs an athletic performance coach. He needs one who is good at what she does and who can at least analyze and understand the demands of volleyball.

Unquestionably, there are some physical and athletic demands that are specifically important to a volleyball athlete. Jumping ability, quick reactions, first-step explosiveness, core strength and stability, landing ability, etc. However, these are not necessarily unique to volleyball.

What a volleyball player needs first and foremost to improve performance and reduce the risk of injury is to improve athleticism and the capacity to express it. Becoming a better all-around athlete and increasing physical qualities will do it.

THE PERFORMANCE COACH

A good sports performance coach is just that: a coach, not a trainer. A trainer gives an athlete exercises, reps, sets, and so forth. A coach teaches while training. She is concerned with getting the athlete to learn physical skills, understand why they are helpful, and improve physically.

Education, both formal and informal, is crucial to a good sports performance coach. Most have at least a bachelor's degree, and today many will have a master's degree. Informal education, including continuing education, internships, and self-study all add to the coach's knowledge. A good coach is passionate about his field and is always looking to learn.

Look for someone with experience that demonstrates she will be able to help. Working with volleyball players, coaching other athletes of the same age and level, or having trained athletes in similar situations would all be relevant experiences.

Every coach has a set of beliefs about what's important in training, health, and fitness. That philosophy should be compatible with one's beliefs. How will you know? Take the time to ask questions.

The coaching style should also be a good fit. If possible, observe the coach working with someone else. How does he instruct, interact, give feedback (and how much)? Does the pace of instruction match you? Does he give enough, too little, or too much information?

HOW TO FIND THE RIGHT COACH

To successfully find a coach who is qualified and a good fit, try looking for a referral. A referral from a person you know or respect will be a better starting point than responding to an ad, searching a list, or picking someone from the local gym.

A good place to start is by talking to knowledgeable volleyball coaches in your area. They may already have firsthand experience working with someone and have had the chance to observe a performance coach's methods and coaching style with their athletes. If a performance coach has a positive relationship with one or more volleyball coaches, she probably has a better appreciation for the game already. Another good option is to talk with the strength coaches at a local university. They may know of someone in your area.

Talking to others in the volleyball community is always a good idea. There may be someone in your area who has experience working with vol-

08

leyball and/or other athletes. Don't limit it to the volleyball community, however; expand your search into the broader athletic community. There may be a great performance coach who has worked with athletes at the level you are looking for but hasn't spent a lot of time with volleyball yet.

You want someone who has some educational background in the field and enough professionalism that she has at least one of the major certifications. These organizations are some of the most respected in performance training:

National Strength and Conditioning Association—NSCA (CSCS certification)
www.nsca-lift.org

National Academy of Sports Medicine—NASM (PES certification)
www.nasm.org

American College of Sports Medicine—ACSM
www.ascm.org

USA Weightlifting—(Sports Performance Coach Certification)
www.usaweightlifting.org

VOLLEYBALL PERFORMANCE PROGRAMS

Several components need to be covered in a volleyball performance program:

INTEGRATION
The program should address these different needs. There are some approaches that seek to build just "core strength," or flexibility, or any one factor, at the expense of developing all these areas. Your program should address all of the areas in an integrated and synergistic way.

CORE
Today you will generally hear about "the core." It refers to the center of the body including the torso and some hip musculature. It is crucial that this area of the body is trained to provide stability, strength, and endurance. It is the link between the upper and lower body and transfers demanding forces crucial to jumping, landing, and hitting in volleyball.

STRENGTH

An athlete needs to build strength in a way that can be used. Since the brain is organized in movements, not muscles, one needs to develop strength with movements. Developing strength through multi-joint, ground-based movements is functional because this can improve the stability of joints and the muscles' ability to generate force. Sitting on a machine, isolating muscles, requires little balance, may reduce coordination between muscles, and can be an inefficient use of time and energy.

Strength is not synonymous with muscle bulk. Muscle can increase strength and stay the same size. While one may need to build some muscle, it should not be the overwhelming goal of the volleyball performance program.

POWER

Power is the combination of strength and speed, the ability to not only generate force but do it quickly. A jump may only involve the feet pushing against the ground for a few hundred milliseconds. Your nervous system has to have the ability to generate as much force against the ground as possible in that time in order to jump higher.

Power is also demonstrated in landing, stopping, and cutting. This is where most noncontact injuries happen, so one needs to work on this deceleration as well as power. If not, it's like taking a car and adding a powerful engine but leaving old, weak brakes. This will end with a crash. Power can be trained with weights, medicine balls, and bodyweight exercises. It's important that it is well addressed.

PREHAB

Steps can be taken to reduce risk of injury. There may be specific risks general for volleyball or risks related to a previous injury. A knowledgeable and experienced coach can help with this.

Knee tendonitis, rotator cuff instability, ankle sprains, and back pain are some of the more common volleyball injuries. Steps can be taken in training to try to reduce risk of these or minimize their impact.

CONDITIONING

Good conditioning, both cardiovascular and muscular, will help one play better and have a good time. It reduces the risk of injuries late in the game, day, or tournament. Done well, it's a performance enhancer. Just make sure the program is balanced so that overuse injuries—doing too much endurance work that repeatedly stress the same body parts in the same way—do not occur.

You can check out Velocity Sports Performance on the Web by visiting www.velocitysp.com/southbay

GAME TIME! KEYS TO ON-THE-COURT SUCCESS

09

What makes the most difference in coaches' effectiveness during competition? There are two areas that must be considered when evaluating your ability to coach, especially during key matches. They are pre-competition preparation and competition concentration and adjustment. These areas are equally important for both the beginning and experienced volleyball coach.

PRE-COMPETITION PREPARATION

Too many times coaches fail to prepare for tournaments or games. As a result, these coaches become reactive and end up flying by the seat of their pants. Most of the important work should be in place before the games begin. The coach and athletes should feel prepared and confident going into the event. The more time spent in preparation,

the less stress there will be during the event. Knowing you did everything you could in preparation for the event gives you and your team an edge.

FOUR KEYS TO EFFECTIVE PREPARATION

1. Skill. Your team needs to master the skills and develop ball control. The fundamentals need to be covered at every practice. You want these techniques to get into the athletes' muscle memory so they will become automatic during the game. You don't want them to doubt their ability to perform a task when it counts the most.

2. Attitude. Your team should be united on attitude. The four areas that need to be reinforced by you are: play well, always try your best, work on improvement, and focus on desire instead of fear. If the team has these attitudes intact, they will become a united force to be dealt with. A lot of teams go into a match with a fear of losing instead of a desire to win. If two teams are equal in skills, it will always be the team with the most desire to win that will be successful.

3. Know Your Athletes. Know what your athletes can and cannot do. Practice situations that put them in predicaments they might find themselves in during games. See how they respond.

4. Organize and Plan. Have a starting lineup with variations. Put all your athletes in "can-do" situations. Develop an optimal game plan for each situation you know they will encounter.

FIVE KEYS TO COMPETITION CONCENTRATION AND ADJUSTMENTS

Once your team has started to play, the basic responsibilities of the coach are surprisingly minimal. The bottom line is that the kids are the ones in control. They play the game. All you can do is call time-outs and make substitutions. However, there are five areas where coaches can help their athletes be successful during the game.

1. Have Total Awareness. Always be aware of what your team is doing, what the opponent is doing, what the referee is doing, and what the score is. Coaches must stay alert. This is no time to be yawning.

2. Adjust to the Opponent. If an opponent is attacking a weakness in your team, you must be able to adjust. For example, if they are serving aces, you must either adjust the receive pattern or make a substitution.

3. Adjust to Your Own Team. There will be times when your team or an individual will surprise you, for better or worse. Be ready to make adjustments from the original game plan.

4. Use Substitutes Effectively. You have twelve substitutions. Use them to help the team and individuals be successful.

5. Use Time-Outs Effectively. You are allowed two time-outs per game. Use them constructively by giving your team information they can use instead of chastising them for their mistakes (they already know about their mistakes). The best times to call time-outs are when the other team has scored three or more straight points, you need to make an adjustment on either defense or offense, or your team appears to be losing their concentration.

WHAT TO BRING TO A GAME OR TOURNAMENT

It's a good idea to make a checklist of what you need to bring to a game or tournament. You don't want to have your team come to you and ask for balls to warm up with and realize you left them at home. The following is a list of items you will need for yourself and your team. You may add to or subtract from this list as needed.

1. Lineup sheets with the players' names and numbers on it
2. Medical release forms for each athlete in case of emergencies (signed by a parent or guardian)
3. A first-aid kit
4. Water for you and your team
5. Pencils or pens
6. Paper or cards for notes on either your team or the opponents
7. A folder to hold papers, lineup sheets, and medical release forms
8. An extra uniform in case a player needs it
9. Volleyballs: one for every two players, marked with your team name
10. Healthy snacks and ice

These are not really secrets, but they are techniques used by some of the most successful coaches. We hear about these things all the time and discount them as being irrelevant or "pie in the sky." However, believe it or not, most of the time they work. Read them carefully and at least consider their potential.

09

PERSISTENCE EQUALS SUCCESS

The greatest secret in the world is: If you really want something, work harder and longer than anyone else. If you want to be a great coach, get as much information as you can. Stop being a frustrated expert and become a student. Don't just choose one coach as a mentor. Look at several and see what techniques work for you and throw away the ones that don't work. If you are willing to put in the time and effort and are persistent, you will eventually be successful. Most people quit before they ever get there.

I remember one coach who came to our practices when we first started our open program. He was just learning how to coach, and he was terrible. When he tried to hit balls at us, the players would make fun of him because he had no control over the ball. We never dreamed he would go anywhere. Well, to our surprise, he persisted and eventually wound up coaching on the national and international level. He is now the head coach at a successful Division I college. Needless to say, we don't make fun of him anymore.

DEVELOP THE CONCEPT OF TEAM

Ask not what your team can do for you; ask what you can do for your team. Even though this is paraphrased from John F. Kennedy, it is very relevant to all team sports, including volleyball. This is especially important with young teams, because kids are used to depending on adults and are not used to people depending on them. To actually be an important part of a group and have the team's success depend on how they perform is a revelation for many kids. Being a part of a team sport and learning how to work with others to make a team great will help kids in future relationships, both personal and professional. If you can convince your kids they should try to help the team instead of vice versa, you will eliminate a lot of selfishness and stress.

I have found that when kids focus on themselves and their concerns, it creates pressure for them. I remember one athlete who called me and complained she was not getting as many sets as some of the other hitters. Both she and her parents were distressed because they felt she was being shortchanged. When they started actually counting how many sets she got in each game, it became apparent that helping the team had slipped her mind. When she was reminded of her responsibilities to the team and the demands of the position she was playing, she backed off and started playing better than ever. She became more concerned about the team and less about herself, and it resulted in her playing better—and eventually she got more sets without even asking. The team concept is one that will enable you to get the most out of your players without a high level of stress. If they are working hard for each other and the team, they will get more out of themselves than if they are only concerned with "I." To pull this off, you must make all the kids feel like they are contributing to the team, de-emphasize individual success, and focus on the "we."

MOTIVATION

We hear this all the time: "My team just doesn't want it" or "If only I could get them to try." These comments indicate a problem with motivation, which can be a difficult area for a coach. What it boils down to is this: It doesn't really matter what a coach wants or what a parent wants. What matters is what the kids want and why they are playing volleyball in the first place.

There are several reasons why kids play volleyball, but the most insidious reason is that someone is forcing them to play. This, unfortunately, is more frequent than we would like to admit. If you have a team made up of players who are playing only to satisfy their parents, you will have a tough time motivating them because they don't have any desire.

If you suspect your team is having motivational problems, it might be helpful to investigate. Take the time to talk to each kid individually. Find out why they are in the sport. What are their goals? How good do they really want to be? Their answers may very well surprise you. If you find out a kid does not want to play, you can talk to the parents, try to talk the kid into enjoying the sport by reminding him of the positive aspects, or release him from the team (with his permission). This may upset the parents, but the kid will be off the hook and will be able to invest time in what he really wants to do.

WORK FOR WHAT YOU WANT

If you have kids who want to be there and really do want to be good, you must educate them that they have to work for what they want. This seems like it would be easy, but a lot of kids are used to getting what they want without working for it. This is a perfect opportunity to teach them that hard work and commitment pay off. Sports do not reward spoiled children. No one will give them a win. They must make a commitment to themselves and the team to be the best they can be. Once the team has a common goal, a hunger will set in. Remember that the desire to win and excel must come from the athletes, not the coach. The coach can only remind them how important it is.

DESIRE VS. FEAR

Once the motivational driving force is there, desire must be accentuated. Too many coaches use fear to motivate their teams. Even though fear is a strong motivator, it is negative and can end up paralyzing players. They become so afraid of the consequences that they back off. They don't want the ball to come to them. Instead, desire should be reinforced. Remind them why they want to win: "I want to help the team; I want to play my best; I want to improve." These are desire-motivated reasons that are a lot better than "I don't want to make a fool of myself; I don't want to make a mistake; I don't want to lose to my friends." Negative reasons such as these for trying to win are self-defeating and will only disrupt concentration and put your team at a distinct disadvantage. I can always tell when a team is afraid of losing to us because they usually beat themselves.

HAVE A POSITIVE ATTITUDE

Once the desire is there, you can either help or hurt your team by your attitude. If coaches are positive about the team and the players, they are more apt to have success than if they are worried about their weaknesses or competition. Positive coaches believe in themselves and their athletes. They prepare for their opponents but do not dwell on them. On the other hand, negative coaches always expect the worst to happen. Since that is what they focus on, they usually lose; it's a self-fulfilling prophecy. All coaches can choose to have a positive attitude. Remember, attitudes are infectious.

MAINTAIN COMPOSURE

Coaches can help their teams by maintaining composure. If a coach is flipping out on the sidelines, it becomes hard for the players to concentrate. As a coach, you are there to help, not distract, your players. If they make an error, don't harass them. Chances are they already feel bad enough. Instead, try to get them to concentrate on the next play. Don't turn one mistake into four. Your athletes need to be confident during the competition; don't be the one who destroys their confidence right when they need it.

POSITIVE CLOSURE

When the game is over, meet with your team before they go home. Regardless of the outcome, if they gave 100 percent effort, let them know you are proud of them. Point out what they did well and what areas still need to be worked on at practice. Ask them for their feedback as well. Have them leave with a positive attitude, which should carry over to the next practice or competition.

ADVERSITY (WHEN BAD THINGS HAPPEN TO GOOD COACHES)

Bad stuff happens. Even if you are a great coach, you will experience adversity. No one is immune. You might lose a close game to an inferior team, have a key player get injured, and so on. What separates coaches aren't the problems but the way the coach handles the problems. A lot of coaches make excuses, and when they run out of excuses, they quit or go to another team. Good coaches accept the challenge and find ways to meet it. They refuse to stay down and usually end up coming back stronger than before. In our society, it is commonly accepted to quit if you don't get what you want. We see this with kids, and we see it with adults. Life is not supposed to be easy and neither are sports. We need challenges to test ourselves. Our kids need them, too. When coaches are faced with challenges, how they react sets an important example for the kids. Adversity makes people work harder and accomplish more. One of my athletes ruptured a disk in her back at the start of the season and could not play for the rest of the year. Obviously, she was very upset. But because of that injury, she was very motivated to come back for the next season and did not take playing for granted. She enjoyed playing more and had her best year ever.

When you experience a setback, instead of wallowing in self-pity or making excuses, use the opportunity as a challenge. It might be just what you need to get your act together.

CLASS

Class is about showing good sportsmanship, taking responsibility for your actions, and being considerate of others. You and your athletes have class if you show pride, humility, poise, and self-confidence without arrogance. If you have class, you never give the impression of being a loser, even if you lose a match. Classy coaches and athletes handle victory and defeat in the same way—graciously with their heads held high. They don't brag in victory or make excuses in defeat. They accept both winning and losing in stride.

Obviously, to have class, you have to put sports in perspective. In the sport of volleyball, too many of our role models have little or no class and showcase arrogance or make fools of themselves when they lose. When kids see these athletes perform, they think this behavior is acceptable and might start emulating these traits.

121

If you want your athletes to demonstrate class, you must show it. You can always recognize coaches with class. They walk out on the court in a confident manner and have their energies directed toward getting the job done and nothing else. They are completely prepared. Their actions speak louder than words. If you have class, you always come off as a winner. If you don't have class, even if you win, you can end up looking like a total loser.

FOCUS ON THE NOW

Now is what matters. When your team is playing, keep them in the present. Don't let them dwell on the past or think about the next game. All that matters is now. This concept will help players concentrate and focus on what they need to do to perform. Each contact of the ball should require their total concentration. Keep this in mind as a coach. What play should you call now? What adjustment will work now? Not only will this concept help in your team's performance, it will make you enjoy what is happening more if you stay in the present. Too many of us dwell on the past (or live in it) or spend all our energy preparing for an upcoming event and don't enjoy or appreciate what is happening now. Really, all we have is the present. This is where we do our living. Don't waste it.

DEVELOPING A COACHING PHILOSOPHY

10

Before you do anything else as a coach, you must understand and develop your own coaching philosophy. Whether you are working with five-year-olds or fifteen-year-olds, a coaching philosophy is needed to provide direction in the important decisions you will make that will affect every member of your team. Basically stated, a philosophy is the why behind what you do. Why are you doing this drill? Why did you take John out of the game? Why is it so important to do the skills correctly? The reasons that back up your actions are important not only to the team members but also their parents. If you haven't done this before, now is the time to develop your philosophy because it will guide your decisions and give you consolation when the going gets tough.

As a coach, you will play an integral role in the personal development of an athlete. Besides teaching the skills and strategy of the sport, you will help kids learn how to deal with life through sports. Life is full of stress, and so are sports. If a child has had a positive experience with volleyball and has learned how to cope with the ups and downs of sports, he will be able to transfer that ability to deal with life and all of its ups and downs. All athletes experience losing and failure at some point in their sports experience. Being able to handle these setbacks should help them in the future when they will have to deal with business, personal relationships, family problems, etc. Athletes are more able to handle losses and setbacks because they have been trained to do so, usually by a coach.

Besides coaching the kids, you will also be a teacher, role model, motivator, disciplinarian, manager, and sometimes a substitute parent. It is very important that every person who chooses to coach is ready to deal with the responsibilities of these roles. As a teacher, you must measure a child's performance by his effort, skill mastery, and contributions to the team, not by the team's winning or losing. As a role model, you must be aware of the fact that what you do is more important than what you say. Remember, little eyes are upon you. Kids will pick up on the behavior traits of their

123

coaches, whether positive or negative. As a motivator, you must get the kids fired up to play. You must be enthusiastic and supportive.

As a disciplinarian, there are times when you must be the bad guy. Kids need to learn how to follow rules, and you are the person who must enforce them. As a manager, you must be able to delegate authority or be prepared to do everything yourself, such as paperwork, registrations, travel arrangements, snacks, etc. In some situations, you will be a substitute parent. Approximately 50 percent of today's athletes are from homes with single parents. And with today's economy, parents have to work hard to make ends meet and are sometimes not there when their kids might need them. You can help by listening and offering helpful advice. If at any time you suspect any sort of parental child abuse, it will be your responsibility to contact law enforcement officers who are trained to handle these problems.

As you can see, coaching involves a lot more than most people realize. To develop your own philosophy, ask yourself these three important questions:

1. Why am I coaching?
2. What do I hope to accomplish this season?
3. What do I want my athletes to say about me in ten years?

WHY AM I COACHING?

When you ask yourself this question, it might take a while to get a response. It seems like a simple question, but if you answer it honestly, you will quickly see whether or not you are cut out for coaching kids.

Here are the top ten reasons why you should want to be a coach:

1. I know this sport and I want to share my expertise.
2. I want to make a difference in someone's life.
3. I enjoy working with kids.
4. I love this sport and want to share my enthusiasm.
5. I want to have fun.
6. I know I can do a good job.
7. I want to be a positive role model.
8. I enjoy being responsible and in charge.
9. I like challenge.
10. I love to teach and see kids improve.

Just as there are positive reasons to coach that will influence whether you are successful and effective, here are the top ten reasons not to coach:

1. I need respect.
2. I want to show off my athletic talents.
3. I want to make money.
4. I want to be famous.
5. I want to make sure my kid is the star.
6. I want everybody to like me.
7. No one else will do it.
8. I need some friends.
9. I want to be in control of others.
10. I think I am a god or goddess.

As you can see from this list, there are a lot of people who are coaching for the wrong reasons. If you chose number five, you might want to immediately read chapter fourteen on coaching your own child. Another reason that is poison is number six. Trust me when I say that, even if you are a great coach, there will always be people who don't like you or how you coach. Some of the best coaches in the world have been the most hated individuals on the planet. The reason is that at times they have had to make unpopular decisions for the good of the team, and you will, too. You must stand by them in the face of criticism. If you just want everybody to like you, you will end up losing control of the team and your self-respect. Politics might be a better choice for a person who has a strong desire to be liked.

After you have honestly identified your reasons for coaching, you must ask yourself another question.

WHAT DO I HOPE TO ACCOMPLISH THIS SEASON?

When you ask most coaches what their goals are for the season, they will say they are aiming for a league title or winning season. Every team has winning as its immediate goal when they are playing; otherwise, no one would keep score. If you're not coaching your team to win, there's something wrong with you. No one tries to lose. The problem with winning comes when it is the only goal or the most important goal. When winning becomes "the only thing," children's sports can become detrimental to the very people they are supposed to help—the kids. The most important lessons don't come from winning. They come from effort and striving to reach one's potential. If you could

125

put yourself into a situation where you knew you would win every game, every time, would that make you happy? Would it make your team happy? I have seen many teams win so much that they didn't enjoy it anymore. I can remember seeing a *Twilight Zone* episode in which the main character found himself in an environment where he won at everything he tried. At first he was thrilled because he thought it was great to win all the time, and everyone was treating him like a god. But soon he came to realize that even when he didn't try, he still won, and eventually even when he tried to lose he kept on winning, which became very distressful. So, the very act of winning at all costs will lose its luster when you take out the effort and the uncertainty of getting there.

Even though there are some exceptions, it is generally perceived that adults value winning more than children. We see this at tournaments when we observe adults watching or coaching children. The behavior of some parents and adult coaches is absolutely intolerable. I sat next to one father who called the girls on his daughter's team "twits" whenever they made a mistake. It was evident he wanted to win the game much more than the girls on the team did. I remember one coach making her team do push-ups every time they made an error. Our team won the match easily because her kids were so sore by the end of the game they couldn't lift their arms above their heads.

In adult-organized youth volleyball, there seems to be a prevalence of stressing winning at the expense of fun. Since our society rewards excellence and success, these values filter into youth volleyball competitions and can sometimes destroy kids. The expectations of the adults are just too high. Most kids have sports in better perspective than adults. Instead of us teaching kids, maybe we should watch the children and learn from them. I remember watching one volleyball tournament in which two youth teams (eleven- and twelve-year-olds) were competing in a very close match. It was an exciting and close contest, and there were a couple of controversial calls on the part of the official. The parents were very vocal at the end of the match and were fighting with the official and among themselves about who really won the game. Outside, the kids from both teams were laughing and playing a game they had made up while their parents were inside fighting. Sometimes, adults act like children when children don't perform like adults. We should all learn to let kids be kids.

Adults tend to seek glory through victory. We see it on television and in the newspaper all the time with college and professional sports. We want a piece of the action, and some adults seek it in coaching youth sports or having a kid in sports. What is the problem? In professional and even some college sports, the athletes are basically paid to entertain us. Is that what youth sports are all about? Is youth volleyball for the benefit and pleasure of adults? If so, we should pay the kids. Otherwise, as adults, we need to get our acts together and give the games back to the kids.

Even though a win-loss record is the most measurable way of determining team success, it surely does not tell you what is happening with your kids. Here are some goals you can achieve, even if you don't have a winning season, that will make a lifelong impact on each athlete on your team. If you focus on these goals, the winning might take care of itself.

1. Help Athletes Master Fundamentals. All sports have basic skills kids should master before they can be expected to play or compete successfully. In volleyball, these skills are serving, passing, setting, spiking, digging, and blocking. Chapter four covers these skills in depth. It is your responsibility to teach the fundamental skills. You must be able to explain the skill, show the skill, observe the athlete, and give appropriate feedback as to whether the athlete is doing the skill properly. This is especially important when working with younger athletes who are learning the skills for the first time. You must be patient and help the athletes correct mistakes while they are learning. It is imperative that athletes are comfortable with their skills, especially before they compete. A well-coached team will execute the fundamental skills with ease and eventually will not even have to consciously think about them. To get your team to this level, you must emphasize fundamentals at every practice and make sure they do the skills correctly. The old saying "practice makes perfect" certainly applies to fundamental training. If, at the end of your season, your athletes can execute the basic skills and haven't developed any bad habits, you have given them a greater gift than any win-loss record. They can take those skills with them to the next season. As far as their win-loss record goes, they have to start over every season.

2. Develop an Athlete's Self-Esteem. Self-esteem is how a person values herself. This area is important when dealing with children and sports, because kids will sometimes tie their self-esteem into either winning or losing. You must prevent this from happening. Self-esteem should not be enhanced by winning or destroyed by losing. It is the effort that is important when developing self-esteem in children participating in sports.

If athletes try their best, they should always be able to feel good about themselves, no matter what the score says. It is your job to remind the athletes that winning or losing will never change who they are. It's how they deal with the win or loss that's important.

If you have a child who has developed positive self-esteem because of your efforts as a coach, you have given that child a lifelong gift that will shine longer than any trophy.

3. Teach Good Sportsmanship. This sounds simple, but you would be amazed at how often this area is ignored. A team has learned good sportsmanship if they show true respect for themselves, their teammates, the officials, and their opponents. Athletes learn this through example. If you model good sportsmanship, chances are your players will learn it from you. The opposite is also true.

4. Learn From Mistakes. According to Elbert Hubbard, "The greatest mistake a person can make is to be afraid of making one." Making mistakes will eventually get an athlete closer to success. It doesn't seem that way at the time, but athletes need to know that making mistakes is a part of learning and growing. I had one athlete on my team who, at the most critical times during a match, would become tentative because she was afraid of making a mistake that would cost us the game. As a result, she was becoming afraid of the ball and was making errors anyway. I told her making an error was okay, as long as she tried to correct it next time. I also told her if she was going to make a mistake to make it a doozy. (In other words, go for it.) She still made mistakes on occasion, but she no longer held back. (The people in the stands started wearing helmets.)

There are more suggestions on coaching goals in chapter nine on the secrets of success. Before you develop a coaching philosophy, you need to ask yourself one more question.

WHAT DO I WANT MY ATHLETES TO SAY ABOUT ME IN TEN YEARS?

One thing is for sure: None of your athletes will remember you for your win-loss record. A coach–athlete relationship is a very special one. In a nutshell, you are preparing children for their futures. Since sports at times are very stressful, you can actually help kids get through some difficult situations that will develop into skills they will use for the rest of their lives. Tolerance, patience, class, respect, and persistence are just a few of the attributes that can make a major difference in the quality of their lives. Most of the time, kids don't appreciate their coaches until they grow up, and then realize they actually learned a lot of things from their coach that had nothing to do with volleyball.

Developing a coaching philosophy is not only important for direction but also for reflection. Unless your team has gone all the way in terms of winning championships, chances are high your season will end with a loss. Don't let your season end there. Remind your kids of all their accomplishments during the season. Have they improved their skills? Were they good teammates? Were they good sports? Did they have fun? Did they gain more confidence in themselves? All of these areas show progress and will be far more important in the long run than any trophy that will only collect dust.

If all you care about as a coach is winning and setting records, you shortchange your-self and your athletes. When you start to head in this direction, you might say these four words to yourself: "All glory is fleeting." However, the impact you have on a child could last a lifetime.

A COACHING CHECKLIST

There are two major misconceptions when it comes to coaching youth volleyball. One is that the only qualification one needs is to have played volleyball in the past. The other is that the better the person played, the better coach he will be. Nothing could be further from the truth. Not only must you know the game and how to teach the skills properly, you must know how to work with kids and their parents. Here are ten important areas in which a person must be proficient if he wants to be a good coach and have a successful program.

1. Patience. Patience is paramount. You must be prepared to say the same thing over and over, and in several different ways. The younger the child, the more patience you must have. What is easy for you to understand and do is rarely easy for a child. Remember, children are starting from step one. It will take time for most children to master the skills necessary to play the game. You might find yourself relearning the skills and breaking them down to the smallest components. In a skill like forearm passing, what are your feet supposed to do? Your knees? Where do you contact the ball? How do you hold your hands? You must be prepared to look at all the skills in this manner so you can direct the child to success. This was probably the biggest adjustment my husband and I had to make when we went from coaching college, national, and professional players to coaching young kids. We naturally thought coaching kids was going to be a lot easier. Boy, were we wrong! Our patience has been (and continues to be) chal-lenged to the max. But the rewards are much greater because when you see a child do something right for the first time, the satisfaction is much greater than seeing someone who already knows how to perform a skill do it in a game.

2. Enthusiasm. You could be the most knowledgeable coach in the world, but if you're not enthusiastic, kids will not learn from you. Remember, kids play sports because they are fun. This is not the time to be overly serious or critical. You must be able to teach the skills correctly, have patience, and somehow make it fun in the process. Does this sound hard? It is! Coaching kids requires a keen sense of humor so kids will learn and enjoy the sport at the same time. If you can honestly develop enthusiasm, not only

129

will your athletes enjoy volleyball more, you will enjoy working with them more. The relationship is symbiotic.

3. Commitment. If you have agreed to coach a youth volleyball team, you must make the necessary time available. This is not a situation where you can do it when you feel like it. One of the responsibilities of coaching is to provide a stable environment for the kids. They should be able to count on you being there. You cannot expect them to make a commitment to you unless you have demonstrated the same to them.

4. Self-Control. You may have gotten away with having a short fuse in the past, but you will definitely not get away with it for long if you are coaching kids. You must learn to take things in stride and continue to remind yourself why you are coaching. However, even if you are the most even-tempered person in the world, you will be tested. I have seen the calmest and most serene people kick balls into the stands, throw tantrums, throw clipboards, break pencils—in other words, totally lose it. The key is to let out the frustrations a little at a time, in a respectable manner. Chapter sixteen deals with stress and is required reading for anyone who has problems in this area.

5. Flexibility. Being flexible means knowing when something is not working and trying to find something else that does. Some coaches force their strategies and techniques on kids and, when it doesn't work, push harder or blame the kids. Remember that all kids are different, so all teams are going to be different from one another. What works with one team might not work with another. This is a great opportunity to open your mind to other styles of coaching. Don't be afraid to try something new on kids. They won't know the difference, especially if it works.

6. A Solid Sense of Values. Honesty, integrity, persistence, kindness, and a sense of cooperation are all important values coaches can teach their athletes through example. Even if you don't want to be a role model, you will be regarded as one by the kids. Children are like big sponges. They absorb the behaviors of people around them. You can see why this is a major problem if you have adults with no values coaching kids. If the coach is dishonest and cheats to win, the kids learn that cheating is okay. It is *never* appropriate for coaches to use their position of power, authority, and celebrity to manipulate, entice, or force athletes into compromising situations or force them to engage in compromising behaviors.

7. Empathy. Do you remember what it was like to be a kid? Do you know what it's like to be a parent and watch your kid play a sport and have absolutely no control?

You need to be able to walk in another person's shoes in order to coach kids effectively. Having a sense of compassion and understanding will help you and all the people with whom you will be dealing.

8. Consistency in Discipline. Even though discipline will be covered in chapter eleven, it needs to be stated that discipline does not work if the coach is not consistent. Hit-and-miss discipline will only disrupt your team. You would be better off with anarchy.

9. Knowledge. Since this will be the first exposure to the sport for some of your athletes, you must know everything and assume they know nothing. Make sure you know the rules and the skills and can explain them to a child.

10. Communication. Coaches must be great communicators. Kids remember what they see more than what they hear. It's not that they can't hear; they're just not listening half the time. Communication is covered in detail in the next chapter.

Coaching youth volleyball can be demanding and challenging. If the only attribute you have is playing experience, you should just keep playing and let someone else coach the kids. Some of the worst youth volleyball coaches have been some of the best players.

A COACHING APTITUDE TEST

Now it is time to test yourself. Answer yes or no to the following questions. At the end of the test, you will see what your coaching aptitude is (or isn't).

1. Do I like being around kids?
2. Can I handle being around parents?
3. Can I handle criticism?
4. Can I teach my athletes to handle criticism?
5. Am I patient?
6. Can I control my anger?
7. Can I be fair and objective when it comes to playing time?
8. Can I make this fun for the kids?
9. Do I know how to teach the fundamentals?
10. Am I competent in handling emergencies?
11. Am I a good role model?

12. Do I know and understand the rules?

13. Can I motivate my team through desire instead of fear?

14. Do I have winning in perspective?

15. Can I teach my team something of value about losing?

16. Do I have a positive attitude?

17. Will I commit to make this a positive experience for every child?

18. Can I treat all my athletes with respect and dignity?

19. Can I enforce rules and be consistent?

20. Can I work on building my kids' self-esteem?

21. Can I teach kids to work together as a team?

22. Am I willing to learn from others in order to be a better coach?

23. Can I communicate with others effectively?

24. Can I handle people not liking me on occasion?

25. Can I make a commitment to my team and be there for all the work-outs and games?

SCORING

If you answered yes to:

All the questions: You certainly will be in demand because you are perfect. (Would you like to coach my team?)

20–24: You definitely have coaching and kids in perspective. Just look at the questions to which you answered no and ask yourself why.

10–19: If you scored in this range, you can still be valuable as a coach but have a lot of areas in which to improve. (You also have a lot of company.)

0–9: If you scored in this range, coaching is not your calling. Working with inanimate objects might be more your style.

FINAL THOUGHTS

In summary, know that you are going to make an impact in the athletes' lives.

We have seen many athletes come back years after we coached them to tell us how much they learned from us. Most of the time, it didn't have anything to do with volleyball. These are the most important lessons. Take the opportunity to make a positive difference in a young athlete.

QUOTES FOR ATHLETES

The following are a few of my favorite quotes from successful coaches who taught their athletes more than a game. Use them if you like to guide you and your athletes.

"The difference between a successful person and others is not a lack of strength, not a lack of knowledge, but rather in a lack of will."
—*Vince Lombardi*

"Do not let what you cannot do interfere with what you can do."
—*John Wooden*

"Winning is not everything—but making the effort to win is."
—*Vince Lombardi*

"Practice without improvement is meaningless."
—*Chuck Knox*

11 COMMUNICATION TIPS AND DISCIPLINE GUIDELINES

To be a great coach, you must be a great communicator. Most of the problems encountered by coaches arise from communication problems. Perhaps the kids don't understand what you are trying to tell them, or they're not listening, or the parents get a distorted version of what you said to their child. To circumvent these problems and help reduce stress, there are some basic communication skills every coach should possess to make the job a little easier.

Have you ever tried to set your car radio to a station only to have it come in fuzzy and unclear? You keep moving the knob to try to hear the music or voices clearly, sometimes to no avail. This is very similar to trying to communicate with young athletes. You must be sure they are receptive or all that they hear or remember will be fuzzy and unclear. But how do you tune into kids? There are no guarantees any kid will register anything you say. Some information will literally go in one ear and out the other, or over the tops of their heads. Sometimes, they will only hear parts of what you said, or they will exaggerate what they heard, which can cause problems when they relay this information to their parents.

Even though there are tremendous variables, here are some suggestions that will come in handy when communicating with kids.

TEN TIPS FOR COMMUNICATING WITH KIDS

1. Make sure they are looking at you when you are trying to communicate with them. Do not let them look down or at the wall or ceiling, at another athlete, or at their parents. You must have eye contact. If they react with their eyes, chances are good that what you are saying is registering.

2. Talk in a calm, firm voice. Some coaches think the only way a kid will listen to anything is if they yell. This rarely works, especially if the coach is yelling all the time.

134

Most kids will tune you out when you start to scream and will not register anything you say. A sure sign of a turn-off is an eye roll.

3. If you want to make sure they get the message, ask them to repeat what you said. If they can't remember, tell them again, and ask them to repeat it again.

4. Be prepared to paraphrase your instructions. Be able to explain whatever you have to say in more than one way, and make it as simple as possible.

5. Use visual aids. Kids will remember what they see more than what they hear. Show them what you want.

6. When correcting athletes, use a combination of praise and criticism. Praise them for effort and any positive steps they have taken before you correct them.

7. Ask them if they have any questions or concerns. Leave the door open for them to communicate with you. Give them permission to speak freely. They might be more likely to listen to you if you listen to them.

8. Focus on the behavior or the skill that is a problem. If athletes are having difficulty with a skill, concentrate on technique and give appropriate feedback until they are successful. Do not make athletes feel inadequate if they are not doing something correctly. Remember, it is your job to make athletes successful. If athletes are having behavior problems, site the specific offense and tell them what you expect and what you will not accept. Be specific. An example would be, "Tardiness hurts the team. From now on we expect you to be on time. The next time you are late you will not be allowed to play the first game of the match."

9. Use "I" or "we" statements whenever possible instead of "you." Phrases like "We need you to concentrate more on your passing" would be more effective than "You need to pass better." Never attack a child's self-esteem. Phrases like "You don't try" or "You're lazy" should never come out of a coach's mouth.

10. Show respect for your athletes and their parents. Even though you may not agree with everything your players and their parents say or do, you must respect what they think and feel. You will only get respect if you give it.

NONVERBAL COMMUNICATION

Besides talking to your athletes, you must also be very aware of your body language and voice inflection. Most communication is not the words we say; it is how we say the words, and our body language. Experts tell us that body language and voice inflection are responsible for 80 to 90 percent of all communication. The words we say only count for less than 10 percent.

Kids take in a lot more visually than they do through their ears. Their sense of sight is much more developed than their sense of hearing, or should I say, listening. They are a lot less likely to tune out what they see than what they hear. A lot of coaches say one thing then act out another. They will tell their teams to be calm and poised, and then do war dances on the sidelines or throw their clipboards to the ground. These are mixed messages. Remember, you are a role model. If you tell the team to be confident but you look scared (because you are), they will see a discrepancy and end up being scared, too. Try to be aware of how you are portraying yourself to your athletes. I remember one of my college athletes who was very tall, strong, and self-assured. She approached me once and told me all I had to do was look at her in a certain way and she was terrified. She called it the "stink eye" and asked me to yell at her instead. I wasn't even aware I had the power to scare a six-foot-tall athlete with a "look." I did use it at times after that with some of my more challenging collegiate athletes. I'm only five foot four. I needed something. But when I started coaching kids, I knew I had to start being more aware of my body language. Kids shouldn't be afraid of their coach.

Be aware of how you say things. Kids are masters of inflection. They will remember how you said something more than what you said. They can imitate you pretty well, too (usually behind your back). Facial expressions and tone of voice will come across a lot stronger than actual spoken words.

Another area to consider in terms of how you say things is sarcasm. Keep in mind that sarcasm does not work with kids. They don't like it, and they don't learn from it. Save it for the adults.

When you have an important message to communicate to the parents, either tell them directly or write it down and make sure they get it. Don't depend on the kids. They might forget or only take half messages home. It's your responsibility to make sure the parents know what's going on.

COACHING TYPES

There are three types of coaches when it comes to communication skills. They are the aggressive coach, the inhibited coach, and the assertive coach.

The Aggressive Coach: Aggressive coaches have an angry, confrontational, and sometimes hostile approach to getting their points across. They are loud, tend to be verbally abusive, and often blame the kids for losses. These coaches will use "you" messages all the time, which usually make kids very defensive. The only bright spot is that aggressive coaches are very entertaining to watch.

The Inhibited Coach: Inhibited coaches tend to be shy and speak too rapidly or in a voice too low to hear. They are not direct and tend to beat around the bush when it comes to problem solving. Body language is weak, with slumped shoulders, and eye contact with the person they are talking to is usually avoided. These coaches fear that they will upset the kids and their parents if they really express general thoughts or feelings. This fear leaves inhibited coaches virtually useless.

The Assertive Coach: Assertive coaches get the point across and, at the same time, respect the rights of others. They speak calmly, directly, and clearly and can maintain direct eye contact. The posture of these coaches is erect and confident.

Which one of these coaches would you aspire to be? I would hope the assertive coach, since this is the only type of coach who will have a positive affect on the kids and enjoy coaching in the process.

BEING HONEST

One final area of communication is honesty. Kids can spot a phony a mile away. Don't make promises you can't keep. If you tell a kid he will start in a certain match and then change your mind, you will lose that kid's trust and respect. Also, if you make a mistake, you need to take responsibility for it. Do not make excuses or blame someone else. Kids need to know you are human, and if you take responsibility for your actions, chances are they will, too. I'm not suggesting you go out and make a bunch of mistakes so your team can watch you own up to them. But since we're not perfect, when we do slip, we should admit it and move on. Remember, you are a role model. Your kids will emulate what you do.

DISCIPLINE GUIDELINES

No one wants to be the bad guy, but you must have discipline on your team. Without it, there will be total chaos. If you don't take charge, the kids or parents will. Being a disciplinarian is never fun, but it is always needed when you work with kids. Children must learn how to follow the rules and accept responsibility for their actions. You are the person who must teach them these important lessons. Having good, consistent discipline on your team may carry over to a kid having good self-discipline in the future.

Too many coaches make the mistake of trying to be a kid's friend instead of an authority figure. By being a buddy instead of a coach, you shortchange your athletes and shirk responsibility. Some coaches are so afraid of being disliked they avoid discipline at all costs. When a problem arises, they either ignore it or let someone else handle it. I know of one coach who desperately wanted her team to like her. She let them do whatever they wanted and invited them over to her house for parties; practices were "play time." She was their buddy, and they all liked her tremendously. But when it was game time, they would not do anything she said. She couldn't understand why they would tell her to shut up when she tried to correct them or make adjustments. Didn't they like her? What happened to this coach is she crossed the line with her athletes. Once you cross the line from an authority figure to buddy, you cannot go back. By trying to be their friend, she gave up control and fostered a situation in which there was a total lack of respect and discipline. She knew a lot about the game, but she did not have enough discipline to be a good coach. Needless to say, her season and her coaching experience were both total disasters.

Here are a few guidelines to help you incorporate discipline on your team. I am not suggesting you need to be a drill sergeant or a heartless dictator to have discipline on your team. But you must be able to enforce rules, have kids take responsibility for their actions, and be consistent with the way you handle problems. You must also realize most kids will test the limits. It goes with the territory. It's like having a bunch of wild horses that test the boundaries of their pen by banging into the fences. Kids will test you and the rules by breaking them periodically, just to see what you will do. You must follow through each time, the way you said you would, or risk losing control of the team.

WHEN IT COMES TO RULES

Wouldn't it just be easier to not have any rules? Yes. It would be much easier, but why would they need you if there weren't any rules? Most youth organizations have set rules they expect both you and your team to follow. Then you usually have your own rules or guidelines you set for the team so they can work together toward common goals. The key to enforcing rules is to not have too many. If you have too many, you run the risk of becoming a nag. Concentrate on the important areas, like being on time, showing respect for teammates and opponents, and letting you know ahead of time if they can't be at a competition. Also, a lot of experts say the kids should set the rules for the team. This may work with an older, more mature team, but most kids don't see any value in rules and therefore won't want any. So chances are good you will be setting the rules.

CONSEQUENCES

Okay, so you have established rules and guidelines for your team. What do you do if a kid on your team breaks a rule? There must be consequences, or the rules become a joke. Consequences involve paying a price. Some consequences are ineffective because they are unfair and usually don't work; others are considered effective because they require players to pay a price and hopefully will discourage the behavior from being repeated.

Ineffective Consequences

The number one consequence most coaches use involves physical activity as punishment. They will make the athletes do extra running or exercises such as push-ups. While this is acceptable to a point, most coaches overuse this type of consequence and run the risk of causing injury and causing children to hate exercise for the rest of their lives. I know of one coach who punishes his kids by making them run around the track until they throw up. Do you think any of these kids will take up jogging in the future?

Another popular consequence involves embarrassing the child. This type of punishment can damage a child's self-esteem. Since all kids are different, you never know who will be severely affected by this technique. I know of one coach who used this method of punishment by making the offenders sing assigned songs with a microphone in front of the whole club. It traumatized one child because she is tone deaf and very sensitive about it. Another child, who was a budding rock star, enjoyed every moment. What was a traumatic experience for one child was an opportunity to show off for another. Stay away from this type of punishment, because you never know how deeply it will affect the athletes, or if it will affect them at all.

Yelling and screaming is another popular method some coaches use to punish their kids. Not only is this embarrassing for the coach, but it is ineffective, especially if the coach does it all the time. After a while, the kids get pretty good at tuning out noise.

Effective Consequences

When it comes to effective consequences, you should ask yourself, "What do kids enjoy the most about sports?" The most common answer is they want to play. This opportunity to play can be taken away from kids if they need to be disciplined. By not being

139

allowed to participate for a certain amount of time, the child will not only pay the price for the infraction but might appreciate the opportunity to participate more and not take it for granted. Give them a time-out and have them sit by themselves while the other kids play. (It helps if the other kids are having fun at the time.) Do not bring attention to the kid. The length of the time-out can be varied depending on the infraction.

Some coaches will ask children what they think might be a fair consequence for breaking a rule. You might be surprised if you use this technique, because sometimes kids will be much harder on themselves than you are. Or you can have them choose a consequence, which gives them a sense of control when paying a price. I did this with one athlete when she broke a major rule. She had the choice of not playing in the next two matches or taking a physical punishment her teammates designed. The physical punishment involved doing extra sprints, sprawling, jumping, etc. She took the physical punishment while her teammates watched. I never had anyone break that rule again.

CONSISTENCY

If you have rules and consequences, you must be consistent about following through, and the rules must be the same for every kid. Some coaches make exceptions when it comes to their stars or their own child. This is poison. Inconsistency will cause a lot of resentment. No one learns anything if you punish some kids and not others.

Remember that all children need discipline. This might be their first experience with having consequences for their behavior since a lot of parents tend to be very lenient. Some children actually crave discipline and might not thank you for it now but perhaps later in life. It is important to have an effective discipline plan for your team. Remember, it's better for your kids to be upset at you than it is for them to be mad at each other. After all, they have to play together. All you have to do is watch.

UNDERSTANDING OFFICIALS 12

Officials control the match. They stop and start every play and make the final decisions on rule interpretations. A coach must be able to accept the official's role when the team is involved in a match and teach the athletes to do the same. This can be difficult at times, because not all officials are alike. Some are good, some are bad, and some are ugly. (The same thing could be said about coaches.) Since you can't control officials, it is important to know how to work with them and understand their points of view. It's all a part of the challenge of coaching.

Officials are human and humans are imperfect, some being more imperfect than others. Most officials referee games for the same reasons you chose to coach. They usually love volleyball and like being around kids. However, they have emotions just like you and will most likely get angry or hurt if they are abused. They also have memories and will most likely remember you and your team if you have made an unfavorable impression.

Believe it or not, all officials are trying to do a good job. Officials don't say to themselves, "I'm going to screw up this match." Why, then, are there conflicts between the official and the coach? For one thing, officials have a different perception of the game than the coach. They are standing in a different place, so they see plays from a different angle. Since they view the game from a different location, they will see some infractions you do not and not be able to see some you do. If there is only one official, that person is bound to miss some infractions because she must follow the ball with her eyes. Also, officials are watching both teams, not just yours. Remember, it's the official's job to referee the game, not yours or your kids' parents. Sometimes parents will volunteer at a moment's notice to offer the official their expert advice, which is never appreciated.

Keep in mind that most officials in volleyball are either volunteers or get very little compensation for officiating. This is not making them rich or famous. Being a referee is usually a thankless job because they do not usually get any feedback unless it is negative. If an official does a good job in your match, it would not hurt to tell him so after the match. He might respond in shock since this happens so rarely.

WHAT MAKES A GOOD OFFICIAL?

Let's take a look at some official profiles from the perspective of a coach. These profiles can help the coach keep things in perspective when the going gets tough. As imperfect as some officials might appear to the coach, we must remember they are a necessary part of the game and an important part of the challenge. We must also remember that officials view coaches in a particular light, and these profiles could easily be refined to describe coaches.

EVALUATION OF OFFICIALS

How can you tell if you have a competent official? Look for these qualities:

1. **Knowledge.** Good officials know the game inside and out. They can always explain a call to your satisfaction.
2. **Consistency.** Ideal officials call the same way every time. If they call the ball-handling skills tight, they will do so for the entire match. There are usually no surprises when the referee blows the whistle.
3. **Quick Reactions.** The alert official stays on top of the game and makes the calls quickly. There is no gap time between the infraction and the sound of the whistle.
4. **Personality.** The best officials know how to deal with people and adversity. They have a sense of humor and can make a difference between a game being fun for everyone involved or being a chore.

Incompetent officials are just the opposite. Their knowledge of the game is questionable, their calls are inconsistent, they make late calls, and are no fun to be around. What is important to remember about having an incompetent official referee your game is that this person is still in control of the match. But you are in control of your team. If you can drill into your team the importance of ball control and emotional control, having the most incompetent official in the world should not affect a well-coached team. A team that lets an incompetent official affect the outcome of the match is not a great team.

THE GOOD

The Perfectionist: This official takes her job very seriously. She knows rules you have never heard of. If you question a call, this referee can make you feel inadequate and stupid. There is no question as to who is in charge here. Go back to your bench.

The Android: This official looks like Data's cousin from *Star Trek: The Next Generation*. There will be times when you will want to check his pulse. The calls come so fast, it's uncanny that anyone has reactions that quick. There is no emotion shown here, and you get the feeling that this person could referee for the next five days straight. If you question a call, you get the feeling that your question does not compute, and the referee thinks you are an irrational creature.

The Happy-Go-Lucky Referee: This official is so gosh darn happy, it's almost unbelievable. She laughs all the time, interacts with the kids and is a pure delight. This person might also be the most incompetent referee you've ever had, but how can you get mad at someone like that? At least they are fun and usually don't affect the game's outcome.

The Blue-Chip Official: This is the official every coach would like to have for every match. This person is very competent, personable, and professional. The game is in control and, in the unlikely event this referee makes a mistake, he will take the responsibility. If you ever complain about this referee, your credibility will suffer tremendously.

THE BAD

The Bumbler: This referee has no clue about what is going on and is in denial. If you question a call, you are ignored, and the referee makes even more mistakes than before. The only consolation is that this referee is usually not competent enough to be biased.

The Defensive Specialist: This official is afraid to look bad. If there is a questionable call, she will take the path of least resistance and try to make up for it on the next play. This referee will blush if you question a call but will never change it, even if it is totally wrong. After a while, this person is compensating so much for bad calls the teams become irrelevant. This referee is competing with herself.

The Biased Referee: This referee takes sides. Close calls will always go in the favor of one team, and if that team is not yours, it can be frustrating. After a while, you might feel the other team has an extra player on it—the one with the whistle. Sometimes a biased official might

143

be a person you recognize. Perhaps this person was an official you harassed in a previous tournament. If an official appears to be biased, there is usually a reason for it. All you can do is focus on your team and, if necessary, inform the tournament director of your concerns.

The Sleeper: This official seems totally inattentive to what is going on. Key calls go unnoticed because the referee was not paying attention. The temptation to pour caffeine down this official's throat is very strong.

The Shotgun Referee: You can tell from the onset that this referee does not want to be there. He keeps looking at a watch or clock to see how much longer he has to stay. This referee will be very quick on the whistle and might start cheering for the team in the lead. Don't plan on going into a tiebreaker game with this official.

The Reactive Referee: This official does not like to have her calls questioned. If you so much as look at her with a questionable look, she will respond with a glare, a sly remark, or put her hand up to keep you from approaching. This referee loves to be in control of a match and at times can make a huge difference in the outcome of a close match. Don't make her mad or expect her to change her calls. The danger is she can shift into a biased referee at any time.

THE UGLY

The Disheveled Referee: This official does not present a professional appearance. He might do an adequate job but does not make a good impression on the players or coaches. Maybe his uniform is dirty and wrinkled, his hair messy, or his hygiene poor. I remember one official who had such bad breath and body odor no one ventured near to question a call. It was just too painful.

HOW TO DEAL WITH OFFICIALS

An official can set off your fight-or-flight response in an instant if you're not careful. This response is primitive and should only be used for life-threatening situations that call for you to either run away or physically fight. A volleyball game is not a life-threatening situation, so you don't need to set off this reaction.

When the official makes a controversial call, immediately take a deep breath, and then close your mouth. The deep breath will bring extra oxygen to your brain where you will then engage your upper power of perception (you have one, trust me). Ask yourself, "Was this really a bad call?" If the answer is yes, you must ask yourself another question: "How bad will this hurt my team?" If the answer is "significantly," you should question the call.

Do not yell or accuse. Instead, ask for a clarification. If you don't get one or do not agree with the explanation, you must realize that how you respond from here will be observed by your players and their parents. Try to stay cool and blow it off. If you blow up, the team might become too distracted to play. Remind yourself and your players that you cannot control the referee; all you can control is yourself. This will hopefully make them focus more on the task at hand, like passing the next ball or serving the next ball in the court.

If handled correctly, a controversial call can motivate your team to play at a higher level. It can be just the impetus the team needs to get the job done. If, on the other hand, you let the official get to you and your team, it will put you at a disadvantage, especially if you start yelling at the official. You don't want an angry official refereeing your kids. This is the formula for creating a biased official.

Don't ever project your loss onto an official. A couple of bad calls should not affect the outcome of the match. Chances are both you and your team made enough errors to contribute to the loss. Mistakes can be ironed out at practice and make your team technically stronger next time. If you blame the loss on the official, you probably won't work on your weaknesses, and you won't be better next time, especially if you have the same official (and chances are good that you will).

There might be times, unless you are perfect, when you will let the official's call get the best of you. Maybe you will throw a clipboard, kick a ball into the stands, or perform unnatural body gyrations. Remember that you are human and might lose control. If and when you do, you should own up to the fact that you were out of line. Let your team know you made a mistake. If you don't, be prepared for your team to start acting like this as well. Players like to know their coaches are human, especially if they admit it on occasion.

Since you are involved in the coaching part of volleyball, chances are you will be asked or expected to officiate on occasion. When this happens, things may look very different to you from the other side of the whistle. The official signs and interpretations follow. Familiarize yourself with these hand signals. Referees don't usually talk to you during a game. You must understand this sign language not only to understand the official but also be able to communicate when you find yourself up on the stand.

OFFICIAL HAND SIGNALS (INDOORS)

These are the most common signals made by officials. All signals that are made with one hand are made on the side of the team that commits the fault or makes the request. After the signal is made, the referee gestures to the player who has committed the fault or the team that has made the request.

Authorization for service **16**	(1) Illegal hit or service (2) Ball not released at time of service (3) Assisted hit **17**	Delay of service (1) 5 seconds (14-and-under) (2) 8 seconds **18**
(1) Served ball does not cross plane of net, or touches teammate, or fails to reach net. (2) Player commits net fault. **19**	(1) Double fault (2) Playover (3) Reserve (14-and-under competition) **20**	Illegal block or screen **21**
(1) Position fault (2) Rotation fault (3) Illegal substitution (4) Improper substitution **22**	(1) Illegal attack beyond the net (2) Illegal block beyond the net. **23**	(1) Illegal attack. (2) Illegal attack of the serve. **24**
Ball contacted more than three times by a team **25**	Individual sanctions: (1) Penalty (2) Expulsion (3) Disqualification **26**	Team sanctions: (1) Team delay warning (2) Team delay penalty warning penalty **27**
Change of courts **28**	Authorization to enter **29**	

13 COACHING AND PARENTS

I feel qualified to write this chapter since I am both a coach and a parent. I have had my share of parent problems as a coach and have also seen my kids coached by others who at times have brought out the worst in me. This chapter will offer insights as to how parents view coaches and their kids. Hopefully, it will not discourage you from coaching kids but make you more aware of the people and feelings you will encounter. If you coach youth volleyball, you will deal with parents. There is no escaping it.

First and foremost, all parents have their children as their top priority; there are few exceptions. If their kid is happy, so are the parents (usually). If the kid is unhappy, the parents are mad. Most of the time, this anger will be directed toward you. Upon observing parents throughout the years (including myself and my husband), I have identified three priorities most parents feel are basic needs when their child is playing a sport:

1. Parents want their child to play. How much? As much as any other kid, especially the ones who play all the time.
2. They want the team to win. Most of the time, they want it more than the kids. Parents are adults, and the very nature of being adults makes them more competitive.
3. They don't want the coach to criticize their child, especially in the company of others.

When you view these priorities as a parent, they look credible, but when you view them as a coach, they look impossible to accomplish unless your program is recreational. First of all, if you are coaching a competitive team and have more than six kids, some of them will naturally play more than others unless you can be successful with them playing an equal amount (which you can't do all the time). Also, even though you coach to win, and teach your kids to try their best to win, there will be times when you will lose. And finally, being critical is part of being a coach; you will be correcting your athletes a lot.

When you coach, it is imperative you communicate your goals and philosophy to both the kids and the parents. Do not try to please parents. Be fair, honest, and firm. Remember, you can please some of the parents all the time, and all of the parents some of the time, but you can never please all of the parents all of the time. It is impossible. If you turn into a parent pleaser, you will lose control of the team. Instead of you coaching the team, they will be telling you what to do.

My husband and I have a simple coaching philosophy. If you'd like to borrow it, be our guest. We identify our program as a competitive one and feel we have three major responsibilities to the kids. First, we try to teach the skills correctly. Second, we try to make the team successful. Third, we play kids where and when they can have the most success. The kids' job is to try their best and support the team. The parents' job is to cheer for their kids and their teammates. That is all. Even though this sounds simple, it is hard for some people to accept, and we always encourage them to leave if our program does not fit their needs.

UNDERSTANDING PARENTS

Parents love their kids and show it in a variety of ways. You are dealing with a great amount of loyalty and love. For this reason, it is very important you communicate with parents and make sure they are aware of your goals and expectations. Have parent meetings, send home notes, and talk on the phone. Do whatever it takes to communicate on a regular basis. Otherwise, when their child complains about the coach and says he is being treated unfairly, how do parents know otherwise? If they understand the rationale behind your coaching, perhaps they could reinforce that with their child. Too often, parents don't understand where coaches are coming from. All they see is an unhappy child.

Believe it or not, parents can offer a lot of support to a youth coach. They want to help. Even though you can't please them all, you can and should ask for their support. One thing is for sure: Kids do not feel good about themselves if the coach is telling them one thing and their parents are telling them another. There needs to be a feeling of unity and understanding for the child to succeed. The coach and the parents need to be part of the same team. Only then will the child be successful.

Another important consideration when dealing with parents is that a lot of them have what I call "blind love." This means they have trouble seeing their child's faults. In volleyball, it means they don't see their child's mistakes. They project it onto another kid (it was Joe's fault, not my son's), make excuses, or blame you (after all, you are

13

the coach). This is important to understand when talking to a parent about a child's performance. You must be objective and have some measure to back up your concerns. No parent will listen to you say his kid is no good, lazy, or can't do this or that. But parents will look at statistics or listen to what their child needs to work on as long as they feel their kid is being critiqued using the same measures you use for every other child. If you favor one kid over another, and have no rational reason for doing so, you will face very angry parents. That makes parents more upset than anything else, especially when their kid is getting the short end of the deal.

Another important consideration when dealing with parents is ego. All people have egos, but when dealing with parents, it is a matter of degree. When you mix a great amount of love with a big ego, you usually have trouble. These parents' moods go up and down with their child's performance. When their child is playing well, they are the happiest people in the world and a lot of fun to be around. If their child is having trouble, they can become very depressed or unpleasant. Understanding this mood swing is a coach's best defense. Do not let it distract you or your players. These people are just being themselves and usually will not change.

Parents can also be very distracting to their kids. This is usually most apparent with younger kids. By the time they are fourteen or fifteen, kids can usually tune out parents pretty well (and you, too). Children love their parents and want to please them. They are terrified of losing their love. All parents will love their kids the same, no matter how they do in a volleyball game (at least that's my belief). Parents assume kids know this as well, but sometimes kids don't feel as secure as we assume. This is why some kids are afraid to compete or lose. They fear they will lose the love and acceptance of their parents and their coach. The way to deal with this is to remind the kids that no matter what happens in a match, their parents will love them the same, as will you as their coach. Smaller children need to be reminded more often, especially if parents are flipping out on the sidelines. If you can see a child is truly distracted by a parent's presence, either tell the child not to look at the parent when she is on the court or ask the parent to move out of the child's sight so she can concentrate. Most parents will understand and comply if they feel it will help their child.

The bottom line in dealing with parents is understanding and communication. They can be your best support system. After all, they have a major vested interest (their child). They can also be your worst enemy and make your life miserable. After all, whose side do you think they're going to choose if it's between you and their kid? (You lose.) Learn how to communicate with parents. Most of the time, they want to be on your side.

FROM A PARENT'S PERSPECTIVE: WHEN IT WORKS AND WHEN IT DOESN'T

By K. Ryan

My husband's and my expectations for involvement in a competitive volley-ball program (both club and school) were that our daughters would learn good skills, the proper way to play the game, and avoid the acquisition of bad habits. We wanted them on a competitive team so they could enjoy success for all of the time and hard work they had put into practices. We hoped that all of the kids and families would get along, creating a pleasant and fun-filled experience with everyone united for the good of the team. We wanted our children to learn sportsmanship, develop a strong work ethic, learn lifelong fitness and health habits, and learn and enjoy a sport they could play for their entire lives.

WHEN IT WORKED

When it worked, we had successful winning seasons with great matches that were so much fun to watch with the team playing great and our daughters contributing in a competitive situation. We made lifelong friendships with fellow parents and had great fun socializing and traveling with them to competitions.

This was a result of the coaches who provided strong leadership, ran organized practices, devised excellent game plans, communicated well with the parents, and kept us involved with the team. It was because the kids were talented athletes, who always gave their best and were wonderful young women and great students and friends. It worked because of the parents who followed through on their commitments to get their kids to practices and games, communicated with coaches in a timely and proper manner when problems arose, cheered for all the kids on the teams and cheered for all great plays, supported one another, and organized "pot luck" meals and snacks at tournaments that the kids really enjoyed.

WHEN IT DIDN'T WORK

There were disappointments and frustrations when our team and/or our daughters got into a slump, when we got to the finals of a tournament and let a championship slip through our fingers, and when there was an incident, situation, or disagreement that caused friction among the team and/or coaches and/or families. It definitely does not work when coaches are controlling and noncommunicative, when athletes or parents are out for themselves, where there is backstabbing and where players who are continually making errors receive extended playing time due to politics or family connections. Rally scoring does not allow leeway for performances, so keeping a player in the game after several mistakes, for whatever reason, is hard to watch and not fair to the team.

FINAL THOUGHTS

It is extremely important to support the coaches and never work against them (except in dire situations). If any problems arise, parents should encourage their children to talk with the coach first before any thought of parent intervention. Be realistic in your expectations for your child. Remember that volleyball is very time consuming for both you and your children. As a parent, you must be willing to be committed to it so that you don't let your child or the team down. As a parent, you must be a team player and be positive. Teach your child and her teammates by example. There should be no "Debbie Downers" or prima donnas. And as a parent, you should never criticize players, especially in front of your child; there is nothing more disruptive to team unity.

Know that even if your child does not play volleyball in college, volleyball may help her get into a better college.

PARENT PROFILES

Even though all parents are different, there are some characteristics that can come out when they are watching their child play sports. You might recognize yourself or others in one or several categories. The most important thing to remember is that parents love their kids and want them to succeed. This is what motivates them to act in peculiar ways. You will only understand this fully if and when you have a child playing sports.

The Gold-Star Parents: These people are 100 percent supportive of you and the team. They will always be positive, no matter what happens. They will cheer for the other kids when their kid isn't playing. If you need help, they will always volunteer but will never get in your way. If you have a problem, they will back you up. The only way you can ever hope to have one or more gold-star parents is if you know what you are doing, interact well with the athletes and parents, and have sports and winning in perspective.

The Critics: These people know it all. They were either all-Americans or watch a lot of television. The critics will be the first to inform you that you don't know what you are doing, especially where their child is concerned. The interesting thing about these people is that they will never volunteer to coach. They would not be able to take the heat. In other words, they can dish it out, but they can't take it.

The Comparison Shoppers: For these parents, the grass is always greener on another team. Their child is on your team, but they spend most of their time watching and comparing your coaching, success, or lack of success to every other team in the gym. Don't count on these parents watching your game if their child is on the bench, not playing well, or your team is losing. They will be on another court, cheering for strangers or interacting with another coach. Be prepared for them to "move on" next season, if not before.

The Wrecks: These parents are a bundle of nerves. They can't stay still during the games and will usually pace up and down the court. Nail biting, hair pulling, and other psychomotor tensions are very noticeable. By the end of the game, they are breathing hard and are usually sweatier than the athletes. It's a good thing your team doesn't play every day. These parents need time to recover before the next competition. (They also make others nervous, including the team.)

13

153

The Frontrunners: These parents identify strongly with winning. Whenever the team is doing well, they are your most visible fans. If, however, the team is losing or not playing well, they will fade into the background or sometimes leave. They do not want to be associated with a losing team.

The Dark Clouds: These parents are perennial pessimists. They see the negative side of everything. If there are any problems on the team, they will make sure you are aware of it. They love being the bearer of bad tidings. It's fun for them to rain on your parade.

The Pollyannas: These parents are the opposite of the Dark Clouds. They are always positive and cheerful, no matter what. You could lose the worst match of your life, and they will find something to be happy about. There is nothing wrong with these parents. They do, however, make you feel like there is something wrong with you.

The Levelers: These parents will put down other kids to make sure their kids look good. Sometimes, they will take stats on other kids so they have proof their kid is better. The sad thing about this is that their comments can get back to the other children and cause a lot of sadness and embarrassment.

The Get-a-Life Parents: These parents are definitely living through their child. They are so concerned about your team winning that you sometimes wonder if their child was conceived for the sole purpose of playing volleyball. At times, they will wear their child's old uniform or their jacket if it has the team's name on it. This enthusiasm is usually harmless unless the parents are enforcing their high expectations on their child. This can be dangerous. I have seen some parents punish their child because he didn't win, even after the coach told the child he played great. I know one parent who grounded his son because he was not named the most valuable player in a tournament. As if the kid had any control over that! You can be helpful by setting the parent straight about the team's goals and reminding mom or dad that this team is for the kids. If they want to play, tell them to go find an adult team.

The Empaths: These parents feel everything their child does during the competition. They make motions with their bodies similar to what their child is doing on the court. Sometimes they will just move their head or arms, but some parents really get into it with their legs, too. They are very alert to what is going on during every play. If their child is running to get a ball, they might be doing the same thing on the sidelines. Too bad you can't substitute these parents into the game, because they are warmed up and ready to go! Some of these parents are also Wrecks and will need extra time off before the next competition.

The Clueless: These parents know nothing about volleyball, and sometimes nothing about sports. They will ask you the most inane questions and will not be able to understand most of what you say. Hang in there. These parents are a lot better to have around than the ones who think they know it all.

The Party Animals: These parents can get totally out of control. They will yell and scream during the entire game and sometimes boo the other team and officials. I have seen officials give these parents red cards and penalize the team for their unruly presence. Sometimes these parents can be under the influence. Guess whose job it is to get these parents under control? You guessed right—yours. You must be tactful and nonthreatening. Make them aware of how their behavior is making the team feel, especially their kid. If all else fails, ask them to leave and later call them when they are in a different frame of mind.

The Rescuers: These parents do not want their children to experience any stress, especially while they are on your team. They will fight all the child's battles and will not let the child take any responsibility for his actions or allow the child to work out any problems with the coach. The parent does all the communicating while the child says nothing. Even though parents must stand up for their children, they must also let their child learn the lessons sports can teach them and learn how to fight their own battles. I would much rather talk to the children about problems they are having with the team than hear it from the parents.

The Airheads (Clueless's Cousins): These parents never register anything in terms of times or dates. Their kid is always late as a result, or sometimes the kid will miss important games because the parents forgot. There will be times when these parents will forget to pick up their kid from practice or forget where practice is. These parents are not doing this intentionally. They are usually overloaded with a lot of other responsibilities. Make sure you communicate with this parent and do not punish the child for their actions, or should I say, lack of actions.

The Perfectionists: These parents expect perfection from you, the team, and especially their kid. Nothing is ever good enough. They will badmouth you and the team constantly because they know of several reasons why you are so incompetent. Even if you win, it will not be by a big enough margin. At time-outs, these parents will coach their own kid and others who are within earshot because what they say is a lot more important than anything you have to say. After the game, they will nag their kid about all of her mistakes. Usually their kid will burn out very quickly in sports because she realizes she cannot be perfect and sports are not fun when mom or dad is there (which is always). The sad thing about these parents is that a lot of them ultimately get into coaching.

The Bribers: These parents will do almost anything to make sure their kid plays all the time in the position they want. Sometimes they are obvious and will take out their wallet and actually say, "I will give you $$$ if you play my kid more." Hopefully, you are not willing to sacrifice your integrity. Some Bribers are not so obvious and may be hard to recognize. These people will take you out to dinner, invite you to parties, buy you gifts, and do favors for you. They will never say why they are doing these things. They assume, that if they do these things for you, you will reward them by playing their child when and where they want. These people can turn into your worst enemies if you don't get the message, but don't give in to them.

The Exhibitionists: These parents love to be in front of a crowd and will take full advantage of every opportunity, which is usually at game time. If there are any cameras around, these parents are not far behind. I know of one woman who, in the middle of a youth doubles beach tournament, went onto the main court between matches and had her kid set her balls so she could spike on the main court. This wouldn't have been too noticeable had she not been in a string bikini. Needless to say, she made quite an impression. These parents are starving for attention. Any kind will do. Don't let them distract your team.

The Volcanoes: These parents can erupt at any moment, for no apparent reason. They will usually explode over the smallest incident. These parents have suppressed so many little stresses you never know when they will blow. You can usually tell these parents are out of line because they will be totally irrational and will not listen to anything you have to say. If it is just you and this person, let the individual go on and just nod. This person will usually call you back later and apologize for the inappropriate behavior. If you have an audience, validate the feelings: "I understand you are upset ..." and try to make another time available when you can discuss the problem. At a later time, the problem will look smaller, and the person will have cooled off. The worst things you can do are going after this person and invalidating him in front of everyone, including the child.

The Self-Assigned Assistant Coaches: These parents look more like the coach of the team than you do. They will be in your team huddle, yell corrections at the players, get on the officials for bad calls, and carry a clipboard. These individuals also wear sweat suits with a volleyball team or volleyball company name on it. They look very official but are usually only one step above clueless. They just like to look important. Tell them to sit down with the other parents.

The Mediators: These parents are your team's link to divine intervention. The mediator will have his hands folded and will sometimes be kneeling during the match. This parent's eyes will look up to heaven, especially when your team makes a mistake. Don't make fun of this soul. If your team starts playing out of this world, you might start to appreciate this individual immensely.

The Rappers: These parents love to talk. The problem is they will only talk about themselves or their children. Nothing else seems to register. Your listening skills and patience will be challenged.

The Backstabbers: These parents are scary. They will be incredibly nice and sweet when they talk to you, but behind your back they are ruthless. Just remember, "sticks and stones ..." You are a coach. You don't need everyone to like you.

The No-Shows: I'd rather deal with any of the above parents than this one. At least you know the other parents care about their kids. They just show it in strange ways. No-shows are never there for the kid. They have more important things to do. This parent's child will watch the other parents cheer for their kids and be there to hug them and brag, or even nag. This child will have nobody but you. Make sure you give these kids a little extra attention because they will need it.

OVERPARENTING

We all love our children and as parents have a strong instinct to protect them. Thus when they are faced with a problem involving a coach, our gut reaction is to step in and resolve the problem for them. When they are faced with difficult skill acquisitions and tasks, we admonish them to "be careful and don't get hurt." Research shows that these instinctive responses may not be in our children's best interests.

These parental interventions send the message that the kids are not capable and need not be responsible, are not accountable for their actions, and there are no consequences for their actions because their parents will take care of things for them. The research suggests that it would be better to follow the old adage: "Never do anything for someone who can do it for himself" lest you enable that person, take away his incentive and drive, and make him dependent. Constantly admonishing kids to "be careful" creates fears in them and destroys the desire to try, take risks, and learn from mistakes.

Finally, due to the fact that we live in a very fast-paced, high-tech society, our kids are engulfed in a world of instant gratification in which they want constant excitement and entertainment. This creates problems for kids that must be overcome if they seek excellence and success in athletics (and in school, work, and life). Skill acquisition and mastery require thousands of repetitions of the same techniques and drills that are not especially entertaining and exciting. Thus the challenges are great for both the athletes and the coach, and parents must understand these challenges.

COACHING YOUR OWN CHILD'S TEAM

14

With volleyball getting more exposure at every level, kids are developing a desire to start playing volleyball at a young age. To provide opportunities for kids to play, some parents start programs and teams for their kids and their friends. When our daughter Teri was ten years old, she expressed a desire to play volleyball on a team. At the time none of the schools or clubs in our area had opportunities for kids that young, so we started our own program. We began with a recreational-instructional program on the beach, which later developed into the Spoilers Volleyball Club, a competitive-instructional program.

Several parents have inquired since then about how to start a volleyball program for their own kids. Getting started is relatively easy. Locate a site, such as the beach or a park, your backyard, or a local gym and begin with a recreational-instructional program (teach and play). Have your child invite the kids they would like to play with, or advertise your program in your local paper and on local bulletin boards. When and if the kids are ready, you can contact the nearest USA Volleyball regional office about how to sign up for tournaments in your area. See the resource guide at the end of this book for the national office phone number and Web site. There are registration and tournament fees, which can be split among the families involved. You will find that there is usually a lot of enthusiasm at the onset of starting a new program. But …

While most people's intentions for coaching are noble, even the best coaches can run into problems. The actual dynamics of coaching a team with your son or daughter on it is the challenging part. First of all, realize that it will definitely change your relationship with your child. The coach-athlete relationship is a special—and stressful—one. There are likely to be great times interspersed with some very hard times. As a coach, you are the one who will be making decisions about who plays where, why, and how often, which will directly affect the kids on the team (your kid's friends), their parents (sometimes your friends), and your kid.

If you can get over these, there are many rewards both you and your child can share. For one thing, you will be spending a lot of quality time with your child and his friends and will have a lot to talk about and share. You will also be in a position where you can influence the quality of the experience that not only your child will have, but the other children as well. Most parents sit and watch helplessly as other people, some of whom have no idea what they should be doing, coach their children. You have an opportunity and a responsibility to make this a valuable experience for both your child and every other child on the team.

PARENT CHALLENGES

Hopefully, you will have parents who are appreciative and supportive of your coaching. The chances of you having great parents are directly related to your communication skills, goals, and ability to treat your kid objectively and their kids fairly.

Some parents can't stand the coach for several reasons. Most of the time this distain stems from the belief that their child is not being treated fairly and your kid is getting preferential treatment. Unfortunately, there are some coaches who are so involved in their child's sports that they are driven to get success for their kid. This will become obvious to other parents when the coach's kid never gets any criticism and the other kids do; the coach's kid is always the star and no one else gets a chance; and the other kids split playing time but the coach's kid is always in there, even if he is not playing well.

It is unfortunate that some coaches do not have any objectivity when it comes to their own child. When awards come along, the coach's kid will get all the attention, even if he doesn't deserve it. As one mother told me, "My kid will never again play for a coach who has a kid on the team. It's just unfair." Some parents will voice their concerns to you if they perceive you are being unfair. But most will keep it inside and just make themselves and their kids miserable. They will talk incessantly behind your back, destroying whatever positive reputation you may have. Prepare yourself for problems with parents. Even if you are treating everyone fairly, remember that they have a very different perception from you (see chapter thirteen).

The way to circumvent parent problems is to first look at your child objectively. This may be the first time you have ever done this, but when you coach a child, you are trying to teach him not just the sport skills but how to work for what he wants. If he doesn't have to work at anything when he plays for you, he's not going to learn anything. Don't use this opportunity to showcase your kid. It will be a temptation at first, because you could probably get away with it if you wanted to. But if you love your kid and want this sports experience to be the very best it can be for her, don't play favorites. If your child wants to play a certain position but doesn't have the skills, give him the same chance you would give another kid with the same skills and give the other kids the same chance you would give your kid. It's the only ethical thing to do.

Another way to understand parents is to imagine yourself in a situation where your kid was not getting a fair shake because of a coach who was favoring his kid. How would that make you feel? You sometimes have to walk in another person's shoes to understand. Make sure you do not become the coach you would hate if the tables were turned.

HOW COACHING AFFECTS YOUR CHILD

The first thing all kids want to know, if they don't already know, is "Who is the coach's kid?" Some kids will want to kiss up to your child to get on your good side. They think that if you treat your child with preferential treatment, maybe you will favor them, too. Other kids may use your child as a target for their displaced aggression. They will not show you their discontent, but they will definitely let your kid know how they feel. Most of the time your child will not tell on her friends because she feels loyalty and doesn't want to be a tattletale. Also, your kid won't want to tell you anything negative because she doesn't want to hurt your feelings. So your kid is really caught in the middle, especially if there is preferential treatment.

COMMUNICATING WITH YOUR SPOUSE

It is very important to communicate with your spouse about your goals and expectations for your child and the team. If your wife or husband is not involved, he or she can be your best support system or turn into a monster. This is your spouse's child, too, and he or she wants what is best for her. Make sure your spouse understands and supports your intentions. Otherwise, he or she can be worse than other parents because you live with this one. You might find that you will be eating by yourself, and most likely you will be sleeping by yourself. It can create an unbearable tension in the home, which will obviously also affect your child.

TIPS FOR COACHING YOUR CHILD'S TEAM

1. Talk to your child about what your role as a coach means and what your philosophy is.
2. Listen to your child's reasons for playing. If he just wants to have fun and be with his friends, make sure you make the program recreational. If your child

wants to be as good as he can be and wants to be on a winning team, your program needs to be competitive.

3. Avoid living through your child. Just because you were a great athlete, or wanted to be, doesn't necessarily mean your kid wants to be, too. If your kid is a great athlete, there is no way you can become one through her.

4. Let your child know he will be treated just like every other child. That includes discipline and skill corrections. Remind him that you are the coach when you are with the team, and that is your job. This job, however, will never diminish how much you love your child. Make sure he knows that.

5. Have a meeting at the start of the season for all the parents and kids where you outline your goals and expectations for the season. Be as professional and caring as possible. Let the parents know you are there to help all the kids.

6. Do not bring problems home. Leave them in the gym. Remember, your kid has to live with you, so don't give her double duty when there are hard times.

7. Find a person who can help you keep a fair perspective. This person should be as objective as possible (probably not your spouse). Usually, other coaches can offer a good support system for each other.

8. Learn as much as you can about your sport. Take seminars, read books, and get as much information as you can about how to coach at your level. This will not only help your team and increase your credibility, but it will increase your child's confidence in you.

9. Never blame a kid for a loss. That includes your kid. There will be a lot of pain associated with this, which is totally unnecessary. If you need to blame someone, blame yourself.

10. Do not put your child at a disadvantage. Some parent-coaches are so afraid of being accused of favoring their kid they end up doing exactly the opposite. The kid will usually get corrected more than the others and will play less than the other kids, even when the team needs her. Even though this is a noble effort on the part of the coach, it is overcompensating behavior, which is unfair to the child.

11. Spend extra time with your kid away from the coaching. Make sure you spend quality time with him when you are just mom or dad.

Treating other kids as you treat your child is the golden rule for coaching a team with your child on it. If you adhere to this philosophy, everyone concerned has the best chance at success and happiness, including you. From our own experiences with coaching our daughters in volleyball, we would like to emphasize that the time spent with your child is worth the hard times. If we weren't coaching them, someone else would, and we probably wouldn't get to see them as much or be as much of a part of their lives. Still, our daughter Teri will tell you there were times when she hated her dad, and our daughter Chrissie didn't like the way her mother rolled her eyes when she coached. No one is perfect!

14

15

INJURIES

These three words should motivate you to read every word in this chapter: "You Are Liable." Even if you don't know the first thing about first aid or athletic training, you are still responsible for every child on your team. It would be wonderful if you had a team doctor or trainer, but most of the time coaches are on their own. Remember that sports involve risk. Injuries happen. Even though volleyball is not a contact sport, some injuries will inevitably occur. Most of these will be minor problems, but coaches need to be prepared for anything. The most terrifying sound you might ever hear is one of your kids in pain after suffering an injury, especially if it could have been prevented. This chapter offers some ways you can safeguard your athletes against most injuries and protect yourself from possible litigation.

The best way to feel competent is to take a first-aid class and a CPR course. Then, should an injury occur, you will know exactly what to do. You will also need medical information on every child on your team. Most youth volleyball organizations require forms to be filled out by the parents before the kids are allowed to practice. If you do not have access to these forms, you can make them up yourself. They should include information about pre-existing medical conditions, any medicine the child might be taking, the name and phone number of the child's doctor, insurance information, and who to call in case of an emergency. There should also be a parent signature to permit medical treatment for the child in case the parent is not present when a child gets hurt and needs immediate care. Your signature or permission will not count for anything. You should also have a first-aid kit handy with ice or an instant ice pack. If you are ever in doubt about how serious an injury is, do not move the athlete. Keep him comfortable until help arrives. Most injuries that occur in volleyball are preventable or easily treatable if the coach takes precautions.

HOW TO PREVENT INJURIES

There are several things a coach can do to minimize or prevent injuries from occurring. If the coach does everything correctly, there is still a risk, but following these guidelines will reduce the probability.

1. Require an Adequate Warm-up. Specific muscles need to be warmed up and stretched before they can be stressed. Cold muscles are like cold taffy—they can rip. If a child comes to practice or a game late, make sure he warms up before he plays. You don't want him doing an explosive move like jumping or sprinting if his muscles are cold. A warm-up could be as simple as jogging lightly around the gym or the court and doing some simple stretches.

2. Teach the Skills Correctly. Fundamentals are not only important to play the game correctly, but they are necessary to prevent injury. In volleyball, when athletes do not have correct footwork, they may start jumping sideways or forward when they should be jumping straight up. Jumping sideways can cause sprained ankles and knee injuries. This is not only a risk for the athlete doing the move incorrectly but also for whoever happens to be close to her. It is your responsibility to teach the basic fundamentals correctly.

3. Use Appropriate First Aid. If you are going to administer first aid, make sure you know what you are doing. Otherwise, wait for the paramedics and keep the child safe and calm. Don't make a child walk around on an injured ankle. Remember, you are not a doctor, so don't act like one.

4. Never Play a Sick or Injured Child. Professional athletes can sometimes play with an injury if they are taped correctly; but they are getting paid. There should never be any reason for you to force a sick or injured kid to play or practice, even if there is parental pressure to do so. If there is pain, swelling, or limitation of movement, the child should not play.

5. Require Proper Playing Equipment. Do not play a child if she is missing a necessary piece of equipment that prevents injuries. Kneepads and athletic shoes are a must. Eventually, as players start to block and jump closer to the net, we recommend they either wear ankle braces or have their ankles taped. Ankle injuries are very common in volleyball, and by taping or using braces they can either be avoided or minimized. (There are some coaches who believe wearing braces or taping the ankles will put the knees more at risk for injury. The research in this area is conflicting. For this reason, we only recommend the use of these braces but do not say that they are required.)

15

165

6. Provide Full-Time Supervision. Make sure you are always present during activity. Kids tend to get crazy when adults are not around and could put each other at risk for injuries. If a child gets hurt at practice and you were not supervising at the time, you can get in more trouble than if the same injury occurred in your presence.

7. Insure Proper Hydration. Coaches need to make sure their athletes get enough water. Dehydration puts athletes at risk of cramps, heat exhaustion, and heatstroke. Also, muscle and tendon tears are more likely to occur if athletes are dehydrated. Never prohibit your players from getting water when they need it.

8. Fix Hazardous Facilities. Coaches need to inspect the playing areas for dangerous conditions. These might include water on the court, wires, glass, or sharp protrusions that could cut players. Do not permit your players to play on the court until it is safe.

9. Do Not Overtrain the Athletes. Some coaches make the mistake of pushing kids past their limits. They overtrain the athletes with the intention of making them stronger but instead end up with a rash of injuries. When kids become sore, tight, and tired, these are signs of overtraining and the coach should consider backing off.

HOW TO TREAT INJURIES

Even the most careful coach will have to deal with injuries. Most will not be serious. Here are some guidelines on how to deal with seven common injuries that can occur in volleyball.

Abrasion (Scrape): Clean the wound with soap and water. Apply an antiseptic cream and cover the wound with a sterile dressing. (These should be in your first-aid kit.)

Laceration (Cut): Stop the bleeding using direct pressure. Use gloves so you don't come in contact with blood. Clean the wound, apply antiseptic cream, and apply a dressing. Use a butterfly bandage if needed. Make sure the child goes to the doctor for possible stitches.

Blisters: If they are closed, do not lance them. Clean the area and apply a sterile dressing, a donut pad, and tape. It they are open, clean the area under the flap around the blisters, and apply an antiseptic cream, dressing, a donut pad, and tape.

Nosebleed: Squeeze the nasal passages and apply ice to the nose and the back of the head. Do not tilt the head back or the athlete might swallow blood. Pack the nose with a gauze roll.

RICE

The next three injuries call for RICE as a first-aid procedure. RICE is an acronym for:

R = Rest. Do not move the injured area.

I = Ice. Ice the injured area for at least twenty minutes to prevent swelling.

C = Compression. Wrap the injured area.

E = Elevation. Raise the injured area above the heart to encourage blood return and limit swelling.

Dislocation (Joint Separation): Calm the athlete. Do not let him look at the injury if possible. Immobilize the dislocation in the position it is found. Do not try to adjust anything! Treat for shock if necessary, use RICE, and have the parents transport the athlete to the hospital or call the paramedics.

Fracture (Broken Bone): Calm the athlete, stop any bleeding, and immobilize the fracture in the position it is found. Treat for shock and use RICE. Have the parents transport the child to the hospital or call the paramedics.

Sprains and Strains (Ligament and Tendon Injuries): Calm the athlete, immobilize the injury, and treat with RICE. Have the athlete see the doctor as soon as possible.

CONDITIONS

These are problems that occur that can effect the functioning of the whole body. They are usually acute (sudden) and can be very severe.

Shock: If an injury is serious, such as a fracture, dislocation, sprain, or heavy bleeding, shock can set in. A coach must be prepared to handle it. When a person is in shock, there is insufficient blood to fill the arteries with enough pressure to supply the body's organs. The signs of shock are increased respiration and heart rate, cold clammy skin, a strong sensation of thirst, and changes in consciousness level. Calm the athlete and stop any bleeding. Lay the athlete down and elevate the feet above the head. If you can find a jacket or blanket, put it over the athlete to prevent chill. Treat any other injury. Have someone call the paramedics.

Loss of Consciousness (Fainting): Open the airway and immediately check for breathing. If the athlete is breathing, wait for help to arrive. If the athlete is not breathing, administer mouth-to-mouth breathing (one breath every five seconds). In conditions where the athlete is not breathing and there is no pulse, someone will need to administer CPR, which involves chest compressions. Only trained individuals should administer CPR. For this reason it is highly recommended that all coaches take a CPR class and become certified.

HEAT DISORDERS

Make sure you are aware of your athletes when it is hot. The athletes carrying the most weight are the most susceptible to heat problems. Make sure your athletes have plenty of water, preferably cold water. If the temperature is over eighty degrees or the humidity is high (over ninety), lighten the practice or hold out susceptible athletes. Never allow your athletes to wear restrictive clothing that would limit cooling. The following problems can result due to heat.

Heat Cramps: These are painful spasms that can occur in any muscle, including the stomach. Have the athlete rest, and apply an ice pack to the area. Have the athlete drink water with crushed ice (if available).

Heat Exhaustion: The athlete will be very weak, dizzy, and sweating profusely. The skin will be pale and the breathing shallow. Get the athlete to a cool area and give cold fluids. If the athlete throws up or faints, get him to a hospital.

Heatstroke: This can be fatal! The athlete will have many of the symptoms of heat exhaustion, except for sweating. She may be staggering or lose consciousness and will have a very high body temperature (above 103 degrees). Try to cool the athlete with ice packs and transport to a hospital ASAP or call the paramedics.

FINAL THOUGHTS

Even though you must attend to your athletes' injuries and conditions, be careful of giving a child too much attention. Instead, concentrate on the injury. If you do give a child a lot of attention she is not accustomed to, it will encourage her to get injured again or possibly fake injuries or illness in the future. We have seen a lot of sports where the injured child is given more recognition for getting injured than for playing well. This can turn a child into a hypochondriac, because most kids love and crave attention. I remember one child before a volleyball game who told her coach that her ankle hurt. The pain kept moving around until it showed up in the opposite ankle. It became very obvious the child just liked the extra attention she was receiving from the coach, parents, and other players who were constantly coddling her.

Remember to never play a child with an injury or an illness. If you adhere to this advice, some of them will get better really soon.

STRESS SURVIVAL TIPS

16

Coaching youth volleyball is not and should not be considered a major life stress. Major stresses are those that threaten our survival. As far as we know, coaching or playing volleyball has never put anyone's life at risk. But the very nature of sport, the challenges of competition, and the frustrations of dealing with kids, officials, and parents can present smaller challenges that can add up and have a general effect on our health. It is important for coaches to know how to deal with problems, put things in perspective, and have effective stress outlets for their own well-being as well as their athletes.

Stress in its simplest definition is our response to change. It is an event that throws us out of our comfort zone and forces us to adapt. The change can either be negative or positive. All animals, including humans, are physiologically equipped to deal with stress. We all have a fight-or-flight response that gets the body ready to either fight or run away. Our adrenal glands secrete adrenaline that releases sugar from our livers for energy, the blood shunts to the muscles, breathing and heart rate increase, and the person is ready for immediate action. Unfortunately, this response is rarely needed in modern times, except for emergency situations. An example would be when a car is coming at you and you must respond quickly to get out of the way. In modern life, most of the events that throw us out of our comfort zone are not life threatening. However, a lot of these events happen every day, and if you coach there will be even more. The challenge is not to set off the fight-or-flight response for every little thing that happens. We need to be selective about what we let bother us. Otherwise, the accumulation of these little stresses will eventually get to us and most likely affect our general well-being. The real key to handling stress is to learn to control it. Avoiding stress or acting like a victim will get you nowhere.

First and foremost, when you coach kids, let your priority be the kids, not yourself. Do not tie your ego into your coaching. I have seen several coaches stressed out because they viewed their team's success or failure as a measure of their self-worth. Not only are they stressed—they infect their kids with stress. Remember, you are there to help the team be successful and help each and every kid improve. When you take your ego out of the picture, an incredible amount of stress goes with it.

When you sense a stressful situation forming, use your higher powers of perception. Remember, this is not life threatening, so you do not have to respond immediately. Take your time and evaluate the situation. If it does not merit your involvement or concern, let it go. Learn how to say "no." If a situation does demand your attention and involvement, use this problem-solving formula:

1. **Stay calm.** Do not allow yourself to get upset right away. Take a couple of deep breaths to get more oxygen to your brain to help with the next step.

2. **Explore and understand the problem.** The problem might be very different from how it is presented to you. You need to take the time to find out what is really happening. This involves asking questions and listening.

3. **Define the problem.** Once you have done some research and soul searching, you will be able to put your finger on what is wrong.

4. **Brainstorm the alternatives.** There are several solutions to each and every problem. Think of all possible solutions even if they seem wild. Write them down.

5. **Evaluate the alternatives.** Take a look at your list and see which ones would work best in your situation.

6. **Choose the best alternative.** After careful consideration on your part, choose the solution you feel is best. Remember that you are in charge of the team and responsible for your decisions.

7. **Take action.** This is where most people foul up. They might go through the previous steps but never do anything about it. You must take action or the problem will stay.

When working with kids and sports there are three short sentences that should always be in the back of your mind to help you keep your perspective:

1. It's only a game.
2. These are kids.
3. I can handle this.

When you find yourself being overcome by the hassles of coaching, remind yourself of these three sentences.

FINDING STRESS OUTLETS

Even if you can solve problems and have situations in perspective, you will still need some stress outlets. Find one or several you think might work for you. The bottom line is that you must learn how to take care of yourself, because no one else will. The following list suggests some possible ways to reduce stress.

TIPS FOR POSITIVE STRESS RELIEF

1. **Exercise.** Any kind will do as long as you enjoy it and are consistent.
2. **Participate in recreational sports.** Sign up for a team and play a game yourself. You should have a lot of pent-up energy from holding back while coaching.
3. **Go out with your friends or your spouse.** You will have just cause to go out and enjoy life.
4. **Get enough rest.** When you coach, a nap is okay, as long as it's not during a competition.
5. **Learn how to relax.** Take time out for yourself. Learn meditation or yoga.
6. **Get a massage.** If you've never had one, just do it.
7. **Take a vacation.** Anywhere will do.
8. **Reward yourself for your efforts.** Don't expect others to reward you.
9. **Go to volleyball matches and watch other coaches.** This is usually very educational and sometimes very entertaining.
10. **Read books and magazines for enjoyment.** They'll help you relax and focus on other things you like.
11. **Take up a hobby that is totally self-indulgent.** Try anything other than volleyball.
12. **Eat a balanced diet.** Make sure you get your essential nutrients.
13. **Delegate authority.** There will be lots of people around who will be willing to help out. Take advantage of this or you will be doing all the work.
14. **Learn from other coaches.** Go to clinics and workshops. Even if you learn just one tip, it will be worth it.

HOW TO HELP YOUR TEAM HANDLE STRESS

The best way to help your athletes handle stress is to emphasize effort and improvement, not winning. If your kids feel they have to win all the time to be valued, they will soon develop a distaste for sports. The effort they put into winning is much more within their

171

control than winning is. Also, if you see a particular child tensing up, remind her of the team's priorities and try to get her to focus on her skills instead of what the score is or what happened previously. Kids will stress out only if the coach allows it.

Remember that volleyball is a game, and it's supposed to be fun! Enjoy your time with these athletes and the sport. The season will be over before you know it, and you cannot go back. Enjoy the present.

AN INTRODUCTION TO BEACH VOLLEYBALL

17

Two-person beach volleyball and six-person indoor volleyball are very similar and, at the same time, very dissimilar. Many of the skills, techniques, and strategies are the same. However, the differences make beach volleyball a very different game. Due to the fact that there are no substitutions and only two players, there is less specialization and, therefore, the need for excellence in all of the volleyball skills becomes essential.

Two players also have to cover the entire court as opposed to six in the indoor game. This creates special problems for the defense and affects the offensive attack tactics. As a result there are important technique modifications and special points of emphasis in the areas of block, drop/peel, dig, get, pass, and attack. Finally, the nature of the game itself—playing in soft and loose sand, playing in the heat and glare of the sun, and playing in varying wind conditions—creates special training and conditioning needs.

SUCCESS IN THE SAND

Success in beach volleyball revolves around the mastery of serving and setting skills. Due to the nature of rally scoring, sideout efficiency is essential, as is the coordination of defensive schemes and transition attacks.

MOVEMENT

Because of the difficulty of movement in the soft and loose sand, it is important to develop proper footwork and movement patterns. These include forward and lateral movement, and most importantly, the ability to open and quickly move back. In addition to acquiring proper movement patterns, it is also imperative to train in the sand to develop "sand legs."

SERVE

Beach volleyball incorporates the use of all types of serves, including the float serve, jump-float serve, top-spin serve, jump serve, sky-ball serve, and reverse sky-ball serve. The direction and velocity of the wind and the angle of the sun play a great role in determining which serve to use.

Serving accuracy is of the utmost importance as well as velocity and consistency. The primary goal of the server is to create serve reception problems so it is difficult for the setter to have a good set.

BLOCK

In two-person beach volleyball, a player may choose to block for several reasons—to score a point, channel the ball to the defender, or slow the ball down so the defender has a chance to run the ball down. Time must be spent and a philosophy developed as to how often to block and when and with what techniques to fake a block and drop to either the line or the angle to play defense.

PASS

Once again, because of the soft and loose sand and the number of players on a team, an adjustment must be made to the serve receive technique. The ball must be passed higher and to the center of the court near the net. When moving forward to pass the short serve, players must be adept at putting a backspin on the ball.

Each person is responsible for half of the court. If the ball is served to the middle, the person who is diagonal from the opposing server passes the ball.

DOUBLES PASSING

DIG AND GET

The goal of the defense is to control the opponent's attack so the transition to offense and scoring of a point can be accomplished. Thus ball control and accuracy of retrieval are essential. Because of the size of the court and the number of defenders, special defensive skills are needed. Players must master the overhand-beach dig, correct wrist work when retrieving the ball underhand, and master the one-hand dig with either hand.

SET

Unlike the indoor game, it is necessary to master both hand and bump setting skills. Often on very windy days, the bump set is by far the most practical and efficient setting form. Otherwise, all things being equal, hand setting provides the setter with the greatest degree of accuracy and control. When a player passes the ball, her partner runs up to the net to be a passing target and sets the hitter. This movement begins even before the ball crosses the net because the team should be able to anticipate who will be passing the served ball.

ATTACK

Two-person beach volleyball utilizes a wider variety of shots and attacks than the six-person indoor game. The soft, loose sand reduces the vertical jump, minimizing the velocity and angle of the hard-driven ball. Players must master hard spikes and

DOUBLES SETTING

DOUBLES SPIKING

off-speed attacks to all areas of the court. The hard spike to the deep middle is an important weapon because it is one of the most difficult to defend.

Being a great spiker on the beach is more a matter of ball control than size and power. The attacking motion must be consistent regardless of which offensive tactic is chosen. Vision of the block and the court must be developed. Use of a varied attack selection gives unpredictability to your offense. Some keys to being a good spiker:

1. Have the same look every time you approach the ball.
2. Develop the ability to hit the ball to any point on the court.
3. Contact the ball as high as possible.
4. To hit power shots, turn your body in the air.
5. To hit soft shots, use your hand and wrist to affect the turn of the ball.

DEFENSIVE SCHEME

Each team must employ a defensive scheme that best suits the skills and abilities of its members. A team composed of small players may choose to not block and work at perfecting strong serving and digging skills and a digging scheme. A team composed of one tall and one short player might choose to specialize with one blocker and one runner. A team composed of adequate-size players can run a defensive scheme that blends blocking and digging tactics of both partners. It is extremely important that both tall and small players learn both the no-block and block/drop games so they can be ready for all partners, opponents, and circumstances.

OFFICIAL BEACH VOLLEYBALL
DOMESTIC COMPETITION REGULATIONS

Beach volleyball for years was played on a sixty-by-thirty-foot court with the sideout scoring method where a team was awarded a point only if they were serving. The games were played to 15 points. Even though this style is still popular, the new game is played on a shorter court, with antennas and a lighter ball, and it uses the rally scoring system. The team that wins the rally scores a point and the right to serve. The games are now played to 21 points unless the match goes to three games, and the last game is played to 15 points. All USA and AAU junior events use the new court and scoring system. The following regulations show how the beach game differs from the indoor game and highlight recent changes in the doubles games. For a full list of the rules, go to www.usavolleyball.org and download the whole rulebook.

THE COURT

The court for open competition measures eight by sixteen meters. The court dimensions for each team's side are eight by eight meters. There are sidelines and end lines but no center-line. The height of the net is seven feet eleven and five-eighths inches for men and seven feet four inches for women. The height of the net may be varied for specific age groups:

	GIRLS	BOYS
Twelve years and under	6' 6¾"	6' 6¾"
Fourteen years and under	6' 11½"	6' 11½"
Sixteen years and under	7' 4⅛"	7' 4⅛"

The antennas limit the crossing space and are considered part of the net. They are fastened to the outer edge of the net on the side bands.

WINNING THE MATCH

The match is won by the team that wins two games. The first two games are rally scoring to 21 points. If the teams are tied, the deciding game is played to 15 points. In the case of a game tie, the game continues until a two-point lead is reached. In rally scoring, whenever a team fails in service, fails to return the ball, or commits a fault, the opposing team wins the rally and a point. If the opposing team was serving, they continue to serve. If they were receiving, they gain the right to serve and also score a point.

SUBSTITUTIONS

There are no substitutions in beach volleyball. If you are playing poorly, prepare to get picked on! If a player gets injured and cannot finish the game, it is forfeited.

SERVING

As in the indoor game, the serve may be played if it touches the net.

TEAM HITS

Each team is entitled to a maximum of three hits before returning the ball over the net. Unlike the indoor game, blocking constitutes a team contact, and any player may make the next contact. The ball may touch any part of the body as long as it is not caught or thrown. The serve may not be received overhand (push pass) as in the indoor game. Also, the set must not be lifted or doubled. However, the ball can be held momentarily overhand with the fingers if used in a defensive action to dig a hard-driven ball.

BEACH COURT DIAGRAM

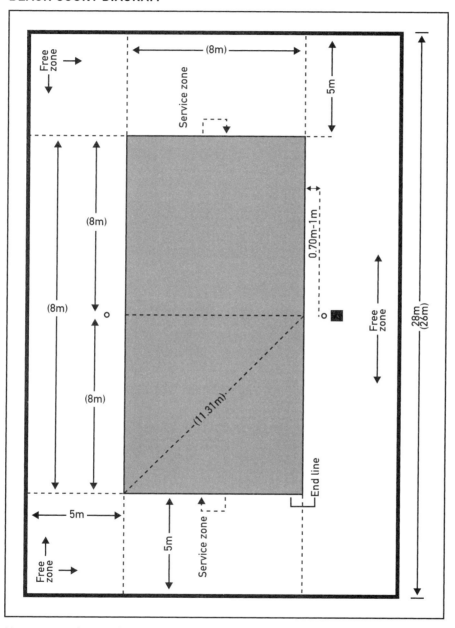

Measurements in parentheses are for Open Competition.

ATTACK HIT FAULTS

There is no open-hand tip allowed in beach volleyball (see indoor tip in chapter four). A player may not use an overhand set to attack if the trajectory is not perpendicular to the line of the shoulders.

BLOCK FAULTS

The blocker may not touch the ball in the opponent's space before the opponent's attack hit. Blocking the serve is not allowed.

TIME-OUTS

Each team is entitled to one-time out per game.

COURT SWITCHES

The teams switch after every 7 points in games one and two; if a third game is necessary, teams switch every 5 points.

TRENDS

It is becoming more common for defenders to return the first ball into open areas of the opponent's court using such techniques as the tomahawk attack, short bump, and long volley. Setters are also beginning to exploit blocking schemes by using a variety of techniques to attack the second ball from the service receive formation. Offensive plays are also being employed to defeat the single blocker. These include attacking various areas along the net, the use of swing and slide techniques by attackers, and the use of different tempo sets by the setters. Finally, coaches are running structured practices that include skill and systems drilling and scrimmage competition.

BEACH-SPECIFIC SKILLS

OVERHAND/OPEN-HAND DIGGING

1. Hands are open; fingers and wrists are stiff.
2. Arms extend to ball.
3. Ball contacts hands.
4. Elbows move forward and under ball.
5. Arms follow through.
6. Wrists remain stiff as ball rebounds off hands.

SKY-BALL SERVE

Step 1: Face sideways with striking hand and arm away from net. Bend knees and drop striking hand back in line with body.

Step 2: Begin to stand up, contacting ball with heel of hand, swinging arm forward and up, chest high.

Step 3: Then turn wrist and palm inward imparting a side-cut on ball, controlling ball with base of palm and follow through with the striking arm.

Note: The best sky-ball serves are sent deep to the opponent's side of the court.

REVERSE SKY-BALL SERVE

Step 1: Begin in bent knee position with striking hand and arm positioned to the net. Bend knees further while dropping the arm of the striking hand and continue bringing striking arm back with elbow locked.

Step 2: Swing striking hand forward contacting ball on top of fist (on muscle between thumb and index finger) throw the ball to chest height.

Step 3: Then turn wrist and palm outward, imparting a side-cut on the ball.

Step 4: Follow through with the striking arm up and the nonstriking arm brought down and back.

ONE-HAND DIG

Step 1: Step at ball with near foot keeping ball inside knee. Get hips under the ball.

Step 2: Reach for ball and make contact with the heel of hand.

Step 3: Point fingers, thumb, and wrist toward target and follow through.

ATTACK

Spiking skills on the beach are similar to those in the indoor game. However, since open-hand tipping is not allowed in the beach game, the off-speed cut shots, roll shots, and high/deep lob shots are essential tools to defeat the defense of the opponent.

On all shots, it is important to jump high and contact the ball high as if to spike it. The approach and arm swing is identical to the spike. The differences are:

HIGH/DEEP LOB SHOT

1. Reach hand up; base of palm contacts bottom of ball.
2. Wrist forcefully and quickly snaps over ball with fingers pointing to desired corner, lobbing ball over defender and deep into corner of court.

ON-HAND CUT SHOT (WHEN STRIKING HAND IS INSIDE THE COURT)

Step 1: Reach hand up and around to inside of ball and contact at the base of thumb.

Step 2: Snap hand and wrist outward with thumb up. Follow through imparting a side-spin on ball.

OFF-HAND CUT SHOT (WHEN STRIKING HAND IS NEAR THE SIDELINE)

Step 1: Reach hand up and around outside of ball and contact ball at base of thumb.

Step 2: Snap little finger, hand, and wrist inward. Follow through sideways with pinky up imparting a sidespin on ball.

17

185

ROLL SHOT

Step 1: Reach hand up; base of palm contacts bottom of ball.

Step 2: Hand, wrist, and fingers roll over ball, arching it over net and blocker and landing behind blocker.

BEACH-SPECIFIC DRILLS

THREE-BALL ATTACK DRILL

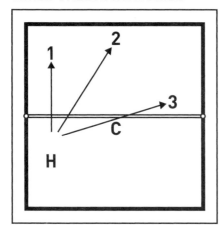

Toss balls to hitter, who hits 1 hard to line, 2 hard to deep middle, and 3 hard to sharp angle. Repeat three times, then repeat with other hitters.

FOUR-BALL SHOT DRILL

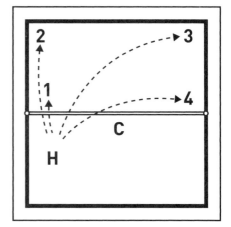

Toss balls to hitter, who rolls 1 over blocker to line, lobs 2 high to line, lobs 3 high to cross-court corner, and cuts 4 sharply crosscourt.

SIDEOUT DRILL

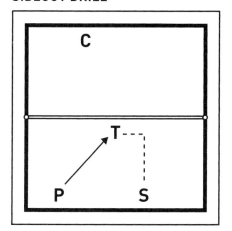

Serve to passer, who passes to center of court. Setter runs to ball at 90-degree angle and sets it. Passer approaches ball, jumps, and attacks it. Five balls are served to one player, then five balls are served to the other player and roles are reversed.

DOWN-TRANSITION DRILL

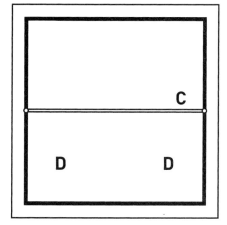

Spike and send balls to all areas of the court. Defenders dig, set, and hit. Repeat ten times, then move to the other side of the court.

BLOCK-TRANSITION DRILL

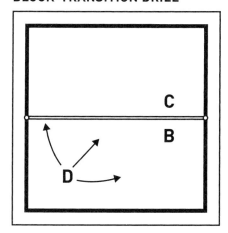

Spike and send balls to all areas of the court. Blocker and defender transition balls. After ten repetitions, move to the other side of court and repeat. If you were on the left, move to the right.

DROP-LINE TRANSITION

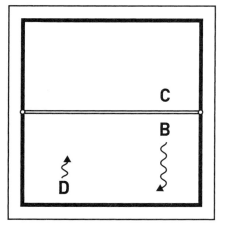

Spike and send balls to all areas of court. Blocker drops to the line; blocker and defender transition balls. Repeat ten times, then move to the other side of court.

DROP-ANGLE TRANSITION

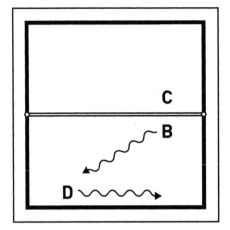

Spike and send balls to all areas of court. Blocker drops to the angle. Blocker and defender transition balls. After ten repetitions move to the other side of the court.

SUMMARY

The beach game is exploding in popularity and has been an Olympic event since 1996. In fact, it is always one of the most attended sporting events at the games. Beach volleyball is a lifestyle sport that anyone at any age can enjoy. Playing volleyball doubles outdoors in the sun, at the beach, the lake, or wherever sand can be brought in is fun and challenging. It is a great opportunity for an athlete to learn and perfect all the skills.

USA and AAU Volleyball now offer several junior tournaments across the nation for kids who want to compete at the highest levels. These events draw hundreds of teams from every part of the country. Check the resources section at the end of the book to find out how to get a schedule. Since 2001, junior teams have been selected to represent the USA in FIVB (Federation of International Volleyball) events around the world. Check with USA Volleyball about the selection process.

Kids love playing on the beach as long as it's fun. As a parent and a coach, if you child wants to play beach volleyball, give her space. You can get her training if she wants to improve her game, but during the matches leave her alone. If a kid has a school coach, a club coach, and a performance coach, the last thing she needs is a beach volleyball coach or parent telling her what to do during a match.

Trust me, your child will figure it out. This sport has all the elements of fun, challenge, and social interaction. Don't turn this game into another pressure for a kid who already might be overloaded. Keep it fun.

AFTERWORD

Research has shown that in order to become a super achiever at any sport, involvement must follow a precise format:

1. Initial motivation for involvement must be *fun*.
2. Eventually that motive will give way to the desire for *recognition and reward*.
3. Finally, motivation becomes *self-actualization* or the need to see how close to perfect one can become.

Note: Steps must follow this precise order or super achievement will not occur.

On Getting Into the Zone: Research has shown that in order to get into the "zone," the skill must be equal to the challenge. When this occurs, performance is effortless and outstanding. When the challenge is too great for skill level, frustration and anxiety follow. When skills are superior to the challenge, boredom follows.

On Winning: When one is committed, both in practice and in competition, to doing his best and to constant improvement, winning takes care of itself. Any other scenario results in underestimating or fearing opponents and growing levels of stress and anxiety.

On Becoming a Champion: Volleyball champions come in all sizes and shapes, with differing levels of quickness, athletic ability, and skill mastery. But all of the great champions have been characterized by these four common qualities:

1. concentration/focus
2. desire
3. discipline
4. extra effort

When they step onto the court, champions are totally focused and centered. They have a singleness of purpose, and their total energy is directed toward success in the present moment. They are not considering future possibilities or past plays—they are totally immersed in the now.

They know that motivation can be fueled by either fear (focusing on the penalties of defeat) or desire (focusing on the rewards of success). They choose to be driven by a burning desire to succeed. They can only comprehend success and its rewards and are determined to get them.

They are hard workers and fierce competitors who know that victory does not always come easy, so they have become disciplined performers. They are patient and persistent and strong willed. They will never quit because they know that as long as they try there is hope; that at any moment the opponent could falter; that victory often will come to the one who has the stronger will.

They demand, expect, and give 100 percent from themselves at all times. They give 100 percent when faced with the seemingly impossible. They give 100 percent when defeat seems imminent, and they give 100 percent even when they have greatly out-distanced an opponent and victory seems certain. They totally prepare themselves for each opponent and each competition. They do more in preparation than others expect of them. They master skill execution, learn their volleyball keys, and develop effective tactics. Champions have two special goals—to improve with each performance and come as close as possible to perfection.

Jamie Grass and Chrissie Zartman: 2001 Silver Medalists, Post Olympics, Under 19, Sydney, Australia Olympic Festival

RESOURCES:
WHERE TO GO FOR HELP

Every coach needs a resource guide to refer to when she needs help finding equipment, uniforms, or information about the sport. The following is a list of companies that are ready to help.

EQUIPMENT

The following companies offer a complete line of volleyball equipment, including shoes, kneepads, uniforms, nets, standards, balls, novelties, books, and videos.

Digital Scout
www.digitalscout.com
3248 West Henderson Road
Columbus, OH 43220
(800) 249-1189

Midwest Volleyball Warehouse
www.midwestvolleyball.com
14050 Judicial Road
Burnsville, MN 55337
(800) 876-8858

Spike Nashbar
www.spikenashbar.com
601 Packard Court
Safety Harbor, FL 34695
(800) SPIKE-IT

VolleyballUSA.com
www.volleyballusa.com
218 Main Street, Unit 802
Kirkland, WA 98033
(800) 494-3933

The Volleyhut
www.volleyhut.com
13955 Stowe Drive
Poway, CA 92064
(858) 486-3307

EDUCATIONAL RESOURCES

The following organizations have information about club and youth volleyball leagues, coaching educational resources, clinics, and volleyball rules.

Amateur Athletic Union (AAU)
www.aausports.org
P.O. Box 22409
Lake Buena Vista, FL 32830
(800) AAU-4USA

**American Volleyball
Coaches Association**
www.avca.org
1227 Lake Plaza Drive, Suite B
Colorado Springs, CO 80906
(719) 576-7777

California Beach Volleyball Association
www.cbva.com
28925 Pacific Coast Highway, Suite 101
Malibu, CA 90265
(800) 350-CBVA

Federation International de Volleyball
www.fivb.org
Avenue de la Gare 12
1000 Lausanne 1
Switzerland

USA Volleyball (the governing body
of volleyball in the United States)
www.usavolleyball.org
715 South Circle Drive
Colorado Springs, CO 80910
(719) 228-6800

Volleyball Canada
www.volleyball.ca
5510 Canotek Road, Suite 202
Gloucester, ON K1J 9J5
Canada
(613) 748-5681

VOLLEYBALL RULES

These organizations provide volleyball rules for high schools and colleges.

**National Association for Girls
& Women in Sports (NAGWS)**
www.aahperd.org/nagws
1900 Association Drive
Reston, VA 20191
(800) 213-7193

**National Federation of State
High School Associations (NFSHSA)**
www.nfhs.com
P.O. Box 361246
Indianapolis, IN 46236
(800) 776-3462

National Collegiate Athletic Association (NCAA)
www.ncaa.com
700 West Washington Street
P.O. Box 6222
Indianapolis, IN 46206
(317) 917-6222

VOLLEYBALL PERIODICALS

Volleyball Magazine
www.volleyballmag.com
Madavor Media, LLC
420 Boylston Street, Fifth Floor
Boston, MA 02116
(617) 536-0100

PROFESSIONAL ORGANIZATIONS

Association of Volleyball Professionals (AVP)
www.avp.com
6100 Center Drive, Ninth Floor
Los Angeles, CA 90045
(310) 426-8000

TRAINING PROGRAMS

These Web sites provide information on specific volleyball training programs.

PlyoCity Youth Development
www.plyocity.com

Spoilers Volleyball
www.spoilersvolleyball.com

Velocity Sports Performance
www.velocitysp.com/southbay
2607 Manhattan Beach Boulevard
Redondo Beach, CA 90278
(310) 297-9001

INDEX

195